Everyday Entertaining

Everyday Entertaining

110+ RECIPES FOR GOING ALL OUT
WHEN YOU'RE STAYING IN

ELIZABETH VAN LIERDE

weldon**owen**

Contents

Do You Want Me to Bring a Side?

'Tis the Season

Lazy Brunch

Treat Yourself!

Introduction

If I'm having you over, chances are you'll be greeted with a strong pomegranate marg and maybe a fun tidbit to amuse your bouche. I'll have a table set up for dinner. Each table setting will be laid out nicely but probably a little mismatched (I'm a sucker for a boho table) and down the center will be an excessive number of lit candles. Fleetwood Mac will be playing in the background and I will have set out too many snacks. I truly love being "hostess" for the night. Having a few hours to take really great care of my people with delicious food and a fun evening is my love language.

I'd love to tell you that I grew up shadowing grandma in the kitchen and absorbing coveted family recipes. But in fact, I remember eating a lot of Shake 'n Bake and Hamburger Helper as a kid.

My first real job after high school was at Williams Sonoma. As I sat waiting for my interview, I suddenly realized that I was not only the youngest person applying but that I sat in a room full of seasoned amateur chefs who had probably memorized every recipe from Ina's newest book and could recite the Le Creuset line by size and color. I was in uncharted waters, seeing as all I could really cook was boxed cake mix. Here's the truth: I was a lost seventeen-year-old going to community college and desperate for a sense of purpose. Luckily, Williams Sonoma gave that to me. The fun cooking gadgets, gorgeous cookware, and unbeatable smells from the test kitchen left me feeling like a fresh sponge ready to soak in everything from the culinary world.

That year I cooked my first Thanksgiving dinner, dressed up as Julia Child for Halloween, and glued myself to cooking shows during any ounce of free time I had. I was completely immersed in my new culinary world. Cooking and learning how to cook gave me a purpose that I greatly needed during this adrift time in my life. I made lavender honey ice cream inspired by the movie *It's Complicated*, and I took homemade macaroni and cheese to whole new levels.

It wasn't until my junior year of college, when I moved into an apartment with roommates, that I was able to really unleash my love for cooking, and most especially cooking for people I loved. Sure, I liked going to class and doing the whole "college experience," but it seemed like my favorite part of the day was always when I got home and threw myself into the kitchen. This was my creative outlet. I'd make seasonal treats for my roommates, cook (what I thought then were) super-elegant dinners like roasted chicken for my boyfriend, Jared, and make myself fancy omelettes every Thursday morning because I didn't have class. In short, I blossomed in my newfound space and quickly realized that cooking for people was easily my favorite extracurricular.

In my spare time I decided to start a food blog. Within a few months I became obsessed with sharing recipes and photos from dinners I was making and small parties we would throw on the weekends. I realized that you could teach yourself how to do anything from a YouTube video or another cook's blog. I loved the idea of sharing easily attainable recipes and ideas that people could put their own spin on for a gathering of their own. Which was ultimately the spark behind this book.

I hope you use this book as a go-to road map for easy everyday entertaining. Everything from at-home happy hours to holiday dinner parties, and every style of gathering in between. Throughout the book you'll find easy menu pairings, simple entertaining items to have on hand, and my go-to staple recipes that I use for my own gatherings. I'll cheer you on as you prep your first Thanksgiving turkey (page 185) and help you whip up an unforgettable miso carbonara (page 131) for your first date night with that special someone.

I knew that when it came to the recipes for this book, I wanted them to be two things: easy yet elevated, and classic for any gathering. My Papa's French onion dip, creamy and incredibly addicting, made an appearance at just about any family get-together we had growing up. Nowadays I might dress it up and down at the same time by serving it with ruffle chips and ice-cold champagne! There isn't a cozy game day that goes by without a double platter of barbecue chicken nachos coming out of my kitchen. In the Cheers! chapter, you'll find out exactly how I make my "jug margaritas" that never have a drop left (hint: you'll use a whole bottle of tequila). They are recipes that are memorable, flavorful, and fit for the moment.

Now more than ever, I have come to realize how precious celebrating with friends and family truly is. As I write this, we are in the middle of a global pandemic, and, unfortunately, throwing my next bash seems like a distant dream. My dinner parties currently include only the members of my household, and happy hour with friends means one or two people, outdoors in the cold, with a mask. Times are just plain weird, and all I can think about are the days to come when I'll be able to open the door and greet my friends into my home. Taking a step back has really taught me that not only should the big events and milestones be celebrated but that the everyday is just as important. Because even if it was a random quarantined Wednesday night, I kept spirits up by turning it into "Hawaiian Night" or "DIY Pizza Night," and this made the ordinary feel intentional and special. Which is what I hope you'll use this book to do.

I am over-the-moon grateful that I am able to offer this book to inspire you and, hopefully, to help you enjoy entertaining as much as I do! Just remember the most important thing to have when you're entertaining is an easygoing attitude. Have fun, don't worry if the cookies burn, everyone is there for great company and a good time. Cheers!

XOXO

EVL

First Kitchen Essentials

Outfitting your first kitchen, or ready to upgrade the essentials? Chances are you've got a few hand-me-down pieces (I was the same!). Don't feel like you need to get everything all at once; if you can check off these items you'll be well on the way to a well-equipped kitchen.

Large Mixing Bowl or Set of Mixing Bowls

They are great for everything from mixing cookie dough to large batches of pasta salad. You always need an extra-large bowl in the kitchen!

Wooden Spoons

Wooden ones are sturdy, they don't conduct heat and burn your hands, and are perfect for taste-testing piping hot sauces and braises.

Measuring Cups

A standard set of dry measuring cups and a glass measuring cup for liquid measurements!

Measuring Spoons

I prefer a stainless-steel option with clearly legible measures on the front of the spoon.

Rubber Spatulas

Great for scraping jars, cleaning batter bowls (who doesn't love a spatula of cookie dough?!), and mixing and folding.

Wooden Cutting Board

Equally as important and partner to the chef's knife. Using a chopping board instead of just chopping on the counter will also help ensure the longevity of your knives (and your counter).

Chef's Knife

The VIP in your kitchen. A great chef's knife can do everything most gadgets can do. It's wise to also have a paring knife for peeling and smaller intricate cuts.

Rimmed Baking Sheets

My rimmed baking sheets get used on the daily for everything from roasting vegetables to baking cookies.

9 x 13-Inch Casserole Dish

My one-pan wonder dish. Perfect for lasagna, enchiladas—you name it.

8- and 10-Inch Skillets

Small- and medium-sized skillets are always on call for things like scrambling eggs, searing meat, making grilled cheese, and more. A set of nonstick, stainless steel or my favorite, cast iron, will be fit for countless cooking uses.

Dutch Oven

There isn't much an enameled cast-iron Dutch oven can't do. Soups, braises, boiling, baking—it's the super hero of the kitchen.

Citrus Press

One word: margaritas.

Entertaining Basics

Whether you're a greenhorn host or a party-throwing machine, these are the essential items you'll need in your entertaining arsenal to get the party rolling.

Plates 6-10

The first essential piece to any solid dinner: a set of great plates. Choose a color that you love or that fits with your other decor for seamless decorating.

Wineglasses

There SO many wineglasses out there, but narrow it down to 1 or 2 sets that you love, preferably on the bigger side! Red and white glasses can totally be interchanged and I bet 9 out of 10 of your guests probably won't know the difference.

Large Shallow Platter

I have one extra-large shallow circular platter that I use for everything! It's amazing for sides and salads, but because it's so shallow you can serve up all of your proteins on it as well.

Flatware

Flatware can be expensive! Invest in a simple set that you love. I would go with a neutral look so you can mix and match with any setting. Gold is classic and timeless.

Cloth Napkins

Cloth napkins?! I know, I know, this might seem like a big step into adult land. But it's necessary and better for the environment! Get yourself a starter set of 8 to 10 napkins (in case you stain one!).

Large Pitcher or Drink Dispenser

Having a premade drink in a pitcher or dispenser will keep your guests busy for that hectic first half hour of any gathering.

A Great Playlist

Even if you don't have any dishes finished, stop what you're doing and turn on some great music before people arrive. This will set an uplifting tone to any gathering.

Wooden Serving Board

Essential for cheese boards, snack boards, and appetizers.

Extras

Birthday Candles
Tablecloth
Candle Holders
Flowers

Alfresco Golden Hour

Having friends over on a warm summer night for an alfresco gathering is magical. An evening filled with insanely easy dishes made with summer produce, endless bottles of wine and Aperol spritzes, and a killer Elton John playlist. In my opinion, there's nothing better.

10-Minute Lemony Herb Cannellini Bean Salad

FOR THE DRESSING

3 tablespoons fresh lemon juice (about 1 lemon)

⅓ cup olive oil

3 cloves garlic, minced

Sea salt and freshly ground black pepper

FOR THE SALAD

2 cans (15 oz each) cannellini beans

1 small shallot, finely diced

⅓ cup minced fresh flat-leaf parsley

1 tablespoon minced fresh rosemary

½-1 teaspoon crushed red pepper flakes

Talk about giving canned beans a face lift. This bean salad is anything but ordinary. Buttery white beans swimming in a zesty lemon dressing and tossed with a plethora of fragrant fresh herbs (use any of your faves!). This is the perfect choice when you're having a grill out and need a quick and healthy side dish.

SERVES 4-6

To make the dressing, in a mason jar or other tightly sealed container, mix together lemon juice, olive oil, minced garlic, and a pinch each of salt and pepper. Shake vigorously for 30 seconds and set aside.

To make the salad, drain the beans into a colander and rinse with cold water. Let the beans drain for 5 minutes, then transfer to a large bowl.

Add the shallot, parsley, rosemary, and red pepper flakes. Season with salt and pepper to taste.

Drizzle beans with three-quarters of the dressing and toss gently. Taste for seasoning, adjusting as needed, and drizzle with remaining dressing just before serving.

Note: Use your favorite herbs! Try basil for fresh Italian flavor or cilantro for Mexican night.

Backyard Steak with Serrano Salsa Verde

FOR THE SERRANO SALSA VERDE

2–3 serrano chiles

1 shallot, roughly chopped

3 cloves garlic

1 bunch fresh cilantro, leaves picked

1 bunch fresh flat-leaf parsley, leaves picked

2 limes, zested and juiced

1 cup olive oil

1 teaspoon kosher salt

2 lb flank steak

Kosher salt and freshly ground black pepper

Grilled healthy meats with zesty sauces are my favorite for summer dinners. This steak takes about 20 minutes to make and is a perfect choice when you're short on time. This flavorful grilled flank steak can be served on its own with fresh side salads like my herby cannellini beans (page 17) or peach panzanella (page 25). This juicy steak also works great diced up in a corn tortilla for an easy taco.

SERVES 4; MAKES 2 CUPS SALSA

To make the salsa verde, in a blender or food processor, pulse serrano chiles, shallot, garlic, cilantro, and parsley until finely chopped. Add in lime zest and juice, olive oil, and salt and pulse until a thick, textured salsa mixture forms. Set aside.

To make the flank steak, pat the steak dry and season liberally with salt and pepper.

Prepare a charcoal or gas grill for direct grilling over medium-high heat. Brush and oil the grill grate. Place the steak on the grill rack directly over the fire. Grill for 2–3 minutes on each side, turning once, until seared on both sides and medium-rare in the middle.

Transfer the steak to a cutting board, tent with foil, and let rest for 5 minutes. Cut across the grain into thin slices and arrange on a platter. Top the steak with the serrano salsa verde, and serve.

Note: Using 2-3 chiles makes a mild salsa verde. Use 3-4 if you want the salsa verde spicier. You can sub in jalapeño chiles if serranos are unavailable.

Make Ahead: Prep the salsa verde the morning of, or up to a few days before serving. Store in an airtight contain in the refrigerator and use within 1 week or freeze for up to 1 month.

Citrus Shrimp with Avocado Crema

FOR THE MARINADE

¼ cup fresh lemon juice

¼ cup fresh orange juice

Zest of 1 lemon

⅓ cup olive oil

1 teaspoon honey

3 cloves garlic, minced

½ cup chopped fresh cilantro

1 lb large shrimp, deveined, shells and tails intact

FOR THE AVOCADO CREMA

1 avocado, pitted and scooped from peel

½ cup Greek yogurt

1 clove garlic

1 tablespoon fresh lime juice

½ cup fresh cilantro leaves + more for garnish

Kosher salt and freshly ground black pepper

All my friends are huge seafood lovers. My favorite thing is putting a flavorful platter of shell-on shrimp with a few ice-cold beers or margaritas in front of them for an easy (and slightly messy) summer appetizer. I know what you're thinking: Shell on?! Yes, girl. Shell on. This keeps your shrimp extremely flavorful and juicy, sort of like shrimp insurance if you accidentally overcook them for a minute of two. If you have any leftover crema, serve it up with chips as a dip, or on top of a taco or any other grilled meat!

SERVES 4 AS AN APPETIZER OR 2 AS A MAIN

To make the marinade, in a small bowl, whisk together lemon juice, orange juice, lemon zest, olive oil, honey, garlic, and cilantro. Pour marinade over shrimp, toss to coat shrimp well, and let marinate for 30–60 minutes.

To make the avocado-cilantro crema, in a food processor, combine the avocado, yogurt, garlic, lime juice, cilantro, 2 teaspoons salt, and a few turns of the pepper mill. Process on high until the crema is smooth and fluffy. Cover with plastic wrap and place in the refrigerator until serving.

Prepare a charcoal or gas grill for direct grilling over medium-high heat. Season shrimp evenly with salt and pepper. Place shrimp on the grill directly over the heat and cook for 2 minutes. Flip shrimp over and cook another 2 minutes, or until shrimp are pink on the outside and creamy white on the inside.

Spread an even layer of the avocado-cilantro crema onto a serving platter and place grilled shrimp on top (or serve on the side). Garnish with cilantro and serve.

Note: These shrimp can also be cooked on a grill pan or in a heavy-bottomed frying pan.

Easy Garlic-White Wine Mussels

2 lb fresh mussels

2 tablespoons olive oil

1 shallot, finely diced

3 cloves garlic, minced

2 small Fresno chiles, thinly sliced

Kosher salt and freshly ground black pepper

2 cups seafood or chicken stock

¾ cup dry white wine

½ cup chopped fresh flat-leaf parsley

1 tablespoon chopped chives, for serving

2 lemon wedges, for serving

Two of my absolute favorite places on earth are Paris, France, and Charleston, South Carolina. If you've been to either, you know that fresh seafood and fries are mandatory and essential for diving into the culture. These mussels are swimming in an aromatic white wine broth and filled with fresh flavors like garlic, Fresno chiles, and chives.

SERVES 4 AS AN APPETIZER OR 2 AS A MAIN

Discard any mussels that do not close to the touch. Prep your mussels by scrubbing them clean and debearding. (Debeard a mussel by grabbing ahold of the string-like filament on the side and firmly pulling down until it's removed.)

In a heavy-bottomed soup pot or Dutch oven over medium heat, heat olive oil. Add in shallot, garlic, and half of the sliced chiles. Cook for 1–2 minutes, or until fragrant. Season with a pinch of salt and a few turns of the pepper mill.

Add in the mussels, stock, and wine. Bring the broth to a simmer, then cover the pot with a tight-fitting lid. Cook for 5–6 minutes, or until all the mussels have opened. Discard any mussels that don't open.

Spoon opened mussels into individual serving bowls, ladle broth on top, and finish with chopped parsley, remaining chiles, chopped chives, and lemon wedges.

Entertaining Note: Skip the shrimp cocktail and try something new and adventurous for your next appetizer. This easy mussel recipe is a fun interactive appetizer that pairs perfectly with hot French fries and cold champagne. You can also serve it with a baguette.

Peach Panzanella with Burrata

⅓ cup olive oil

¼ cup red wine vinegar

2 cloves garlic, minced

1 teaspoon Dijon mustard

Kosher salt and freshly ground black pepper

FOR THE SALAD

3 tablespoons olive oil + more for drizzling

1 small baguette, ciabatta, or Sperlonga loaf, cut into 1-inch pieces (about 8–10 cups)

Kosher salt and freshly ground black pepper

2 medium heirloom or Roma tomatoes, cut into 1-inch cubes

2 Persian cucumbers, cut into ½-inch pieces

½ small red onion, thinly sliced

2 medium peaches, sliced

1 cup fresh basil leaves, thinly sliced and loosely packed + whole leaves for topping

4–8 oz (1–2 balls) fresh burrata cheese, cut open

Peach panzanella is a flavorful bread salad that is brimming with juicy summer produce and laced with a simple, zesty vinaigrette. I'd literally soak up this vinaigrette with just dry crusty bread if it was all I had in the house, it's that delish. Feel free to use up random produce and stale bread but do NOT skimp on the burrata! This soft Italian cow's milk cheese with a creamy center can be found in most grocery stores these days, but fresh mozzarella makes for a delicious substitution.

SERVES 6–8 AS A SIDE

To make the dressing, in a large bowl, whisk together olive oil, vinegar, garlic, Dijon mustard, ½ teaspoon salt, and a few turns of the pepper mill. Whisk until the dressing is emulsified and smooth.

To make the salad, in a large sauté pan over medium heat, heat the olive oil. Add the bread, a pinch of salt, and a few turns of the pepper mill. Turning frequently, toast for 8–10 minutes, or until bread cubes are golden brown. Set bread cubes aside and let cool.

To the large bowl with dressing, add in toasted baguette pieces, tomatoes, cucumbers, red onion, peaches, and sliced basil. Toss gently until everything is well coated. Season to taste with salt and pepper.

To assemble the salad, transfer the salad to a serving platter, place the cut burrata ball in the center of the salad, drizzle with olive oil and garnish with basil leaves.

Entertaining Note: Feel free to swap any fresh stone fruit or different kinds of tomatoes into this versatile summer salad.

Grilled Pizza

FOR THE DOUGH

1 packet (2¼ teaspoons)
active dry yeast

1¼ cups warm water
(105–110°F)

4 cups all-purpose flour

2 tablespoons olive oil + more
for pans

1 tablespoon honey

1 teaspoon sea salt

FOR THE PIZZA TOPPINGS

2 cups store-bought red
pizza sauce

16 oz fresh mozzarella cheese,
thinly sliced

1 jalapeño chile, thinly sliced

6 oz soppressata or
spicy pepperoni

½ cup Simple Pesto (page 30)

Crushed red pepper flakes

Fresh basil leaves

Even if your house is the party house, you still need some easy tricks up your sleeve for those last-minute get-togethers. Throw out lots of cold beer, wine, and an array of toppings, and let people DIY their own pizza. If you're feeling really cheesy (pun intended), make a contest out of who can make the best pie.

MAKES 2 MEDIUM PIZZAS

To make the dough, in the bowl of a stand mixer fitted with the dough hook attachment, combine yeast and warm water. Stir together until the mixture is foamy and pale in color. Let sit for 1–2 minutes to activate yeast.

To the water and yeast mixture add in flour, olive oil, honey, and salt. Begin to knead the dough with the dough hook for 7 minutes. The dough can also be kneaded by hand on a lightly floured surface for 8–10 minutes, or until the dough is smooth, silky, and elastic. If your dough is still sticky, add in 1 tablespoon of flour at a time until the texture becomes smooth.

Grease a large baking sheet or two bowls. Divide the dough into two separate balls and brush with olive oil. Cover the dough with a kitchen towel and place dough in a warm, dry area for 1–2 hours to rise. (My mom always placed our pizza dough covered with a towel in an unheated oven for a perfect rise in a non-drafty area!) If you plan to use only one dough ball, let the pizza dough rise fully and then place into a lock-top bag or an airtight container. The dough will keep in the refrigerator for up to a week and the freezer for up to 3 months.

The dough should double in size. After the rise, flour your hands and a surface, punch down the dough, and begin to press the air bubbles out of the dough. Shape it into an 8- to 10-inch disk about ¼ inch thick. Place dough onto a parchment-lined tray drizzled with olive oil to prevent sticking. Brush the top of the dough with olive oil.

Brush and clean your grill grates. Preheat grill to 425–450°F. Ready your toppings and place onto a tray that can be taken outside easily. You will begin to top and work quickly once the dough is added to the grill.

To place the dough on the grill, flip the dough onto the grill with the parchment side up. Peel the parchment and close the grill. Cook for 2–3 minutes, or until the bottom of the pizza dough is charred and slightly brown and the top is slightly bubbling.

Flip the pizza dough with a large spatula and tongs. Begin to quickly and safely top your pizza evenly with sauce, mozzarella cheese, jalapeños, and soppressata. Close the grill lid and cook for an additional 3–4 minutes, or until cheese starts to become melted and bubbly.

Remove pizza with tongs and a large spatula and place onto a large cutting board to cool for a few minutes. Drizzle pizza with pesto and sprinkle with red pepper flakes and basil leaves before cutting into slices and serving.

Baking Methods: Alternatively, this pizza could be made in a traditional pizza oven and baked for 7–8 minutes at 500°F, or in an oven on a pizza stone or sheet pan at 425°F for 10–15 minutes, or until the crust is golden brown and the cheese is melted and bubbly.

Side Notes: You could easily use store-bought pizza dough if you don't have time to make it. The grill is great for making pizza because it can usually get hotter than your regular oven, and the best pizza comes from the hottest ovens.

How to Grill a Whole Fish

1 wild-caught red snapper (about 2–3 lb), cleaned and scaled

Olive oil

Kosher salt and freshly ground black pepper

½ bunch fresh rosemary

½ bunch fresh flat-leaf parsley + small sprigs for serving

4 cloves garlic, peeled and sliced in half

1 lemon, thinly sliced

Tip: Pair this fish with Simple Sophisticated Greens (page 42) and herby Cannellini Bean Salad (page 17) for a summer dinner alfresco.

If the thought of cooking a whole fish intimidates you, pour yourself a glass of white wine and dismiss any scary thoughts down the drain. You got this. The trick is to let your fishmonger do most of the work for you by cleaning, deboning, and scaling it. After that, it's as easy as bringing it home, seasoning well with plenty of herbs, garlic, and salt, and grilling until you have crispy skin perfection.

SERVES 4

With a sharp knife, cut 3 diagonal cuts down to the bone on each side of the fish. Drizzle an even layer of olive oil onto each side of the fish. Sprinkle 4 teaspoons kosher salt and a generous amount of pepper in an even layer on both sides of fish and inside of the cavity.

Stuff the cavity with rosemary, parsley, half the garlic, and half the lemon slices. Wedge remaining garlic into diagonal cuts on outside skin.

Prepare a charcoal or gas grill for direct grilling over medium-high heat (400–500°F).

Grill fish until skin is blistered on the first side and not sticking to the grates, 12–15 minutes for red snapper.

Using a large, long spatula, carefully flip fish. Be assertive and do your best to glide the spatula underneath the fish in one quick movement.

Continue to grill until skin is blistered on the second side and flesh is opaque and easily flakes with a fork, about 10–12 more minutes.

Grill remaining lemon slices for 1–2 minutes, or until charred.

Remove fish from grill and tent with foil for 5 minutes. Top with charred lemon slices and extra herbs for serving.

Side Note: When purchasing your whole fish, be sure to have your fishmonger clean, gut, and scale your fish. (This doesn't cost anything extra and they are happy to help you.) Your fish will be 90 percent prepared at this point. In the words of Ina Garten: "How easy is that?"

Simple Pesto

1½ cups fresh basil leaves

4 cloves garlic

¼ cup pine nuts

½ cup grated Parmesan cheese

Kosher salt and freshly ground black pepper

½ cup olive oil

During the summer months, I put pesto on EVERYTHING. Grilled meats, fish, pizza, roasted veggies, pasta salads, you name it. Pesto brightens up the simplest of meals with its fresh flavor and bright color. I love making a batch with fresh basil from our little backyard garden and using it throughout the week. My all-time favorite way to use this pesto is in my recipe for Salmon with Pesto & Blistered Tomatoes (page 33).

MAKES 1½ CUPS

In the bowl of a food processor fitted with the blade attachment, combine the basil, garlic, pine nuts, Parmesan, ¼ teaspoon kosher salt, and a few turns of the pepper mill, and pulse until coarse. With the motor running on low, drizzle in the olive oil. Season to taste with more salt and pepper, if needed.

Store in an airtight container in the refrigerator for up to 1 week or in the freezer for 3 months.

Note: For a more modern take, swap in any of your favorite nuts or try a combo of tender herbs such as mint or cilantro, or tender bitter greens like arugula.

Entertaining Note: If you need to throw together an outdoor dinner fast, grill up something easy like chicken or shrimp and serve with a dollop of pesto right on top.

Salmon with Pesto & Blistered Tomatoes

1 lb mixed cherry tomatoes

3 cloves garlic, minced

Kosher salt and freshly ground black pepper

3 tablespoons olive oil

1 large (1–1½ lb) center-cut salmon fillet or 4 small fillets (3–4 oz each)

1 cup Simple Pesto (page 30)

This is my tried-and-true go-to fish dish for dinner parties. I have made this dozens of times, with never an ounce of salmon left, ever. My favorite part about this dish is that I can prep absolutely everything the morning of, pop it into the refrigerator, and just bake it off before people arrive. It's the most unfussy, delicious meal that will leave everyone asking for the recipe. Serve with plenty of crisp rosé, fresh bread, and a green side.

SERVES 4

Preheat oven to 425°F.

Line a small baking sheet with parchment paper. Toss together the cherry tomatoes, garlic, and a sprinkling of salt and pepper. Bake for 15–16 minutes, or until cherry tomatoes have burst and are slightly browned.

Line a separate baking sheet with parchment paper and set aside. Brush a light coat of olive oil onto salmon fillet(s) and season with salt and pepper.

Bake for 10 minutes, then spoon 1–2 tablespoons of pesto evenly over salmon fillet(s). Bake for an additional 2–3 minutes, or until the salmon flakes off easily when prodded with a fork.

Gently place salmon fillet(s) onto a serving platter and top with burst tomatoes.

Note: If you don't love salmon, you can replace it with cod or halibut.

Spritz it up!

5 WAYS TO APEROL SPRITZ

My favorite way to start a summer Friday evening: an aperitif on the patio.

1. The Classic

1 fl oz Aperol • 3 fl oz prosecco • Club soda for topping (optional) • Orange wedge

Fill a large wineglass with ice. Add Aperol to glass and top with prosecco. Stir together until combined. If desired, top with the soda for a lighter taste. Garnish with with an orange wedge.

Note: I'm not a fan of adding soda water, but if you want a true authentic spritz, this is just how the Italians make them!

MAKES 1 COCKTAIL

2. The Negroni Spritz

1 fl oz Campari • ½ fl oz vermouth • 3 fl oz prosecco • Green olives

Fill a lowball glass with ice. Add Campari and vermouth and top with prosecco. Stir together until combined. Garnish with olives.

MAKES 1 COCKTAIL

3.

5.

3. The Pineapple Rosé Spritz

1 fl oz Aperol • 2 fl oz pineapple juice • 3 fl oz rosé wine • Club soda (optional)
Pineapple wedge and leaves

Crush enough ice to fill a large wineglass. Add the Aperol and pineapple juice to the glass of crushed ice and top with rosé wine. Stir together until combined. If desired, top with club soda for a lighter taste. Garnish with a pineapple wedge and leaf.

MAKES 1 COCKTAIL

4. Aperol & Tonic

1 fl oz Aperol • 1 fl oz gin • 3 fl oz tonic water • Cucumber ribbon • Blackberry

Fill a coupe glass with ice. Add Aperol and gin to glass. Top with tonic water and stir well. Garnish with a cucumber ribbon and blackberry.

MAKES 1 COCKTAIL

5. Frozen Spritz

10 fl oz Aperol, frozen • 12 fl oz orange juice, frozen • 2 cups frozen strawberries
1 bottle of prosecco • 2 cups ice • Orange and grapefruit slices to garnish

In a blender, combine frozen Aperol, frozen orange juice, strawberries, Prosecco, and 2 cups of ice. Blend on medium speed for 30–60 seconds, or until smooth and frothy. Pour into large wineglasses and top with orange and grapefruit slices.

Note: Freeze Aperol and orange juice in ice cube trays the night before or at least 4 hours before making. The Aperol won't freeze entirely, but will become semi-firm.

Entertaining Note: I love blending these 30–60 minutes before people are coming over and just popping the blender into the freezer until serving time!

MAKES 4–6 COCKTAILS

Stone Fruit Crisp 3 Ways

FRUIT FLAVORS

Strawberry and Nectarine

Blackberry and Plum

Cherry and Apricot

FOR THE FILLING

6–8 cups fruit of choice
(4–5 cups stone fruit,
2–3 cups berries)

⅔–1 cup granulated sugar

2 teaspoons cinnamon

Zest of 1 lemon

Juice of ½ lemon

5 tablespoons cornstarch

FOR THE CRUMBLE TOPPING

½ cup brown sugar

¾ cup all-purpose flour

½ cup rolled oats

1 teaspoon cinnamon

1 teaspoon salt

½ cup (1 stick) cold unsalted butter, shredded (see Note)

Vanilla ice cream, for serving

If there is one dessert I make more than any other during the summer, it's a stone fruit crisp. A crisp has a "lazy girl" attitude: she's ready in a quarter of the time of a pie, but is just as, if not more, delicious. Use any stone fruit in season—peaches, plums, apricots—along with fresh berries for a dessert that is oozing with fresh summer flavor. Whatever you do, don't skip the scoops of vanilla ice cream.

MAKES 4-6 SERVINGS

Preheat oven to 375°F.

To make the filling, taste test fruit for sweetness; if fruit is very sweet, start with just ⅔ cup sugar, and increase accordingly depending on tartness. In a large bowl, combine all fruit, sugar as needed, cinnamon, lemon zest, lemon juice, and cornstarch. Stir well and let fruit macerate while making the crumble topping.

To make the topping, in a separate medium bowl, combine the brown sugar, flour, oats, cinnamon, salt, and butter. Crumble together with your hands or with a pastry blender, until mixture is sandy and crumbles are about a nickel size.

Transfer fruit mixture to a medium casserole dish or cast-iron frying pan. Top evenly with crumble topping and bake uncovered for 35–45 minutes, or until top is golden brown and fruit is bubbly on the edges. Serve warm, with a scoop of ice cream.

Note: Using a cheese grater to grate your butter helps your crumble topping come together in five minutes or less!

Entertaining Tip: You can assemble the crisp ahead of time, wrap it up tightly, and refrigerate until baking the morning of or the night before serving.

Summer-Soaked Honey Berries with Whipped Cream & Pistachios

FOR THE BERRIES

6 oz blackberries

6 oz raspberries

6 oz blueberries

1 lb strawberries, hulled and halved

¼–½ cup honey

Zest and juice of 1 lemon

1 handful torn mint leaves

FOR THE WHIPPED CREAM

1 cup heavy cream

2 tablespoons sugar

Chopped or whole pistachios

Sometimes during unbearable hot summer nights (like the nights you just want to stand by the freezer) all I want for dessert is something extremely fresh like a bowl of watermelon or fresh summer berries. These berries are glazed with a simple honey-lemon sauce, and topped with fresh whipped cream and chopped pistachios (or any of your favorite nuts!).

SERVES 4-6

To make the berries, in a large bowl, gently toss together blackberries, raspberries, blueberries, strawberries, honey, lemon zest and juice, and mint leaves with a wooden spoon or rubber spatula. I like to start small with the honey and taste test for more as needed. Serve immediately, or cover and place in the refrigerator until serving.

To make the whipped cream, in another bowl, combine cream and sugar. Using a hand mixer, whip the cream on high speed until soft peaks begin to form when whisk is lifted.

Spoon berries into small bowls or cups, and top with whipped cream and a handful of pistachios.

Entertaining Notes: These berries are also the perfect topper for instant summer sangrias or fresh lemonade. To make the prep even easier, make these berries ahead of time, pop them in the refrigerator, and use store-bought whipped cream.

Simple Sophisticated Greens

6–8 cups mixed salad greens

2 small Persian cucumbers, thinly sliced

Juice of 1 lemon

2 tablespoons olive oil

Kosher salt and freshly ground black pepper

Parmesan cheese, shaved

Some entrées shine on their own and just need a simple salad served alongside. Add any vegetable or topping to these salad greens to give them your own spin, or serve them as is and let the ingredients shine. Depending on what I'm serving, I'll swap out the lemon juice for balsamic vinegar or white wine vinegar.

SERVES 2-4

If salad leaves are large, gently tear them into the serving bowl. Add in thinly sliced cucumbers. Drizzle greens with lemon juice, olive oil, ¼ teaspoon kosher salt, and a few turns of the pepper mill.

Top with freshly shaved Parmesan cheese and mix well until greens are well coated with dressing. Serve immediately.

There isn't a summer that goes by where I don't set up a huge dining table in the middle of my small backyard for dinner with our closest friends. You see, this kind of entertainment can be set up anywhere. A space big or small can handle the most balmy of summer nights. All you need are some candles, great wine, and three or four dishes to serve family style. My alfresco menu go-to's: an oyster platter, pesto salmon with blistered tomatoes, ten-minute herby cannellini bean salad, and honey-soaked berries with plenty of fresh whipped cream.

Boards & Platters

A great cheese board or platter takes an evening a long way. It acts as a satisfying starter if you're running late with a meal, sets the tone for what's to come, and can honestly be a meal in itself for two, paired with your favorite wine or cocktail.

Anatomy of a Classic Cheese Board

CHEESES

Pick a blend of 3–5 cheeses ranging from soft to hard.

SOFT: Burrata, mozzarella, Brie, Saint-André (my favorite), Humboldt Fog

SEMI-SOFT: Stilton, Gorgonzola, goat cheese, Gouda

SEMI-HARD: Manchego, Swiss, provolone, Comté

HARD: Aged Cheddar, Parmesan, pecorino, Asiago

FRESH FRUITS

Grapes (green and red), figs, apples, berries, apricots, peaches

DRIED FRUITS

Cherries, apricots, figs, apples, mango

Cook's Tip:
Your cheeses will have more flavor if you let them come to room temperature for 20–30 minutes before serving!

I often get asked if I ever want to open a restaurant. My answer: sort of?! I'd love to open up a cute charcuterie shop where people can pick and choose everything for their own customized cheese board. A sort of glorified happy hour spot to officially decompress, with delicious cocktails and funky cheese to get the night started. Use this easy guide to create your very own classic cheese board.

CURED MEAT

Prosciutto, salami, calabrese, Varzi salami

BRINY THINGS

Cornichons, olives, artichokes, sun-dried tomatoes

BREAD & CRACKERS

Baguette, tiny toasts, breadsticks, multigrain crisps, water crackers

SPREADS

Honey, fig spread, preserves, chutney, apple butter

NUTS

Pecans, pistachios, almonds, Marcona almonds, cashews

Farmers' Market Board with Whipped Honey Goat Cheese

FOR THE WHIPPED HONEY
GOAT CHEESE

4 oz goat cheese

¼ cup plain Greek yogurt

2 tablespoons honey

Sea salt

Olives

Marcona almonds

Peaches, sliced

Plums, sliced

Grapes on the stem

Figs, halved

Baby cucumbers, sliced

Endive leaves, torn

Whole young carrots

Crackers or toasts (optional)

Sometimes during my Saturday trip to our local farmers' market I'm hyped up on one too many iced almond milk lattes and I literally buy everything delicious in sight. To help me go through all my fresh produce, I love putting together an easy mixed crudité board with delectable tangy goat cheese dip that tastes delicious with anything you dip in it! Serve with chilled rosé.

SERVES 4-6

To make the whipped honey goat cheese, combine goat cheese, yogurt, honey, and a pinch of salt in a food processor. Blend until smooth and creamy. Taste test for salt and adjust accordingly. Spoon into a shallow bowl and place in the center of a large rectangular serving board. (Whipped goat cheese can be kept in an airtight container for 3-4 days in the refrigerator.)

Place olives and Marcona almonds in small bowls. Arrange fruits, vegetables, and crackers (if using) around your board.

French Fry Platter with Homemade Dipping Sauces

FOR "THE SAUCE"

½ cup mayonnaise

¼ cup ketchup

½ teaspoon Worcestershire sauce

½ teaspoon freshly ground black pepper

1 teaspoon garlic powder

1 teaspoon Old Bay or Cajun seasoning

½ teaspoon cayenne pepper

FOR THE KETCHUP

1 can (6 oz) tomato paste

⅓ cup brown sugar, honey, or agave nectar

⅛ teaspoon kosher salt

½ teaspoon cayenne pepper

½ teaspoon garlic powder

1 tablespoon apple cider vinegar

¼ cup water

FOR THE HERBY RANCH DRESSING

¼ cup buttermilk

1 cup mayonnaise

½ teaspoon fresh lemon juice

⅓ cup chopped fresh herbs (such as dill, parsley, and/or chives)

1 teaspoon garlic powder

½ teaspoon onion powder

Kosher salt and freshly ground black pepper

FOR THE FRIES

¼ lb frozen crinkle-cut fries

¼ lb frozen waffle-cut fries

¼ lb frozen curly fries

¼ lb frozen tater tots

There isn't one of my friends that won't tell you I'm obsessed with ketchup. Sometimes I joke about getting a small packet of ketchup tattooed on my body (it would be kind of cute, no?!). Ketchup is by far my favorite condiment, and I always order extra, especially with french fries. Simple as this idea may be, whenever I put down this french fry platter with homemade dipping sauces, it's almost impossible for anyone to turn this universal favorite food away. Pick and choose your favorite fries and make just one or all three of the dipping sauces for serving.

SERVES 4-6

To make "The Sauce," in a small bowl, whisk together mayonnaise, ketchup, Worcestershire sauce, black pepper, garlic powder, Old Bay seasoning, and cayenne until well combined. Cover and refrigerate for at least a half an hour before serving to allow the flavors to come together.

To make the ketchup, in a small saucepan, combine tomato paste, brown sugar, salt, cayenne, garlic powder, vinegar, and water. Place over medium heat and whisk until smooth. Bring mixture to a low boil, reduce the heat to low, and simmer for 10–15 minutes, stirring often. If the mixture becomes too thick, thin out with 1 tablespoon water at a time.

Remove ketchup from heat and let cool to room temp. Add water in 1 tablespoon increments until you have your desired consistency. Transfer to a jar or covered container to chill.

To make the Herby Ranch Dressing, in a small bowl, whisk together buttermilk, mayonnaise, lemon juice, herbs, garlic powder, and onion powder. Taste test for salt and pepper and season accordingly.

Spread frozen fries and tater tots onto a large baking sheet in an even layer and bake according to package instructions. (The rule of thumb is 425°F for about 25–30 minutes.)

Put dipping sauces in small bowls and arrange on a serving platter. Arrange warm fries on platter and serve immediately.

Mezze Platter

FOR THE HUMMUS

Juice of 1 lemon

¼ cup tahini

1 clove garlic, roughly chopped

1½ tablespoons olive oil

Kosher salt

1 can (15 oz) chickpeas, drained, rinsed, and peeled (see Cook's Tip)

FOR SERVING

1 bunch baby carrots or carrot sticks

½ head celery, chopped

2 Persian cucumbers, sliced in half

1–2 beets, thinly sliced

1 Belgian endive, leaves torn

1 bunch radishes

½ cup peperoncinis

Pita bread, cut into triangles

Great hummus is tangy, savory, and downright addicting, while still being healthy and good for you. Is hummus even real?! Once you start making hummus at home, it's hard to turn back to any store-bought variety. This pantry staple recipe is perfect for serving up as an afternoon snack, healthy lunch, or alongside Greek Meatball Bites (page 77) for happy hour.

SERVES 4-6

To make the hummus, in a food processor, combine lemon juice, tahini, garlic, olive oil, and ½ teaspoon salt. Blend for 30 seconds, or until the mixture is very smooth and creamy. Add in half the chickpeas and blend for 30 seconds. Scrape down the sides of the workbowl with a rubber spatula, add in remaining chickpeas, and blend until thick and smooth, 1–2 minutes.

If the hummus is very thick, slowly stream in 1–2 tablespoons of cold water at a time until a creamy consistency is achieved. Taste test for salt. (Store hummus in an airtight container for up to 1 week in the refrigerator.)

To serve, place hummus into a shallow serving bowl and drizzle with olive oil. Place onto a medium serving platter and arrange vegetables and pita slices evenly.

Cook's Tip: While it may seem tedious, taking the peels off your chickpeas will make all the difference for your hummus. Challenge your roommate or partner to a contest and see who can shell them the fastest. Winner buys the first round of drinks at dinner.

An Unintimidating Oyster Platter

FOR THE MIGNONETTE SAUCE

⅔ cup champagne vinegar, red wine vinegar, or white wine vinegar

2 tablespoons minced shallot

Kosher salt and freshly ground black pepper

24 fresh oysters

Cocktail sauce, store bought

1 lemon, cut into wedges

Hot sauce (optional)

There is something so special about serving up an oyster platter at home. Usually ordered at a coastal restaurant, it can quite easily be made in your kitchen and served in your backyard. I love handing over a few oyster knives and letting the guys go at them. The trick is buying the freshest oysters possible and serving them chilled on a platter of ice with plenty of mignonette sauce and lemon wedges.

SERVES 6–8

To make the mignonette sauce, in a small serving bowl, mix together vinegar, shallot, and salt and pepper to taste. Cover and refrigerate until serving.

Scrub and rinse oysters under cold running water before serving. To open oysters, hold each oyster in your less dominant hand wrapped in a cloth towel, with flat top shell facing up. Slip an oyster knife into the hinge connecting the two shells, keeping the knife close to the top of the shell to cut the muscle. Twist knife to open the oyster and remove any small bits of shell around the edge. Be careful not to tip the oyster juices out of the shell. Oysters should smell salty and briny like the sea; discard any that are concerning. Run the knife gently along the bottom shell to detach oyster from shell.

Place oysters on a large platter of crushed ice. Fill two other small bowls with mignonette sauce and cocktail sauce. Arrange bowls of sauce and lemon wedges around oysters and serve immediately, with hot sauce (if using).

Mexican Beer Snack Board

BEER

Modelo

Pacifico

Tecate

Corona

FRUIT

Pineapple wedges

Mangoes, cubed

Orange slices

Lime wedges

Watermelon wedges

Cucumber spears

SNACKS, CANDIES & CONDIMENTS

Tortilla chips / Guerrero Tostadas, broken

Takis Stix (spicy corn snacks)

Chicharrones de harina (fried Mexican wheel crisps)

Cooked shrimp, threaded onto spears

Hot chile peppers

Chile nut mixture, store bought

Peperoncinis

Mara Mango (spicy mango lollipops)

Tarugos Tamarindo con Chile (Mexican tamarind candy sticks)

Chamoy (chile-apricot glaze)

Tajín (chile-lime seasoning salt)

Tapatio hot sauce

Growing up in Southern California, I had friends with all different backgrounds. Often the most Caucasian kid in my friend group, I was introduced to some incomparable Mexican cuisine. Whether it was a pit stop after school for an afternoon piece of candy or a large shopping trip on Saturday for carne asada night, Mexican markets were a staple in our grocery rotation. I can still feel my mouth on fire from the first time my friend Sabrina gave me a bag of Takis. Branch out a little and try some new flavors from your local Mexican market, you won't be disappointed!

SERVES 4-6

Grab a large takeout box or cardboard box and trim the sides down. Position a cold 6-pack of your favorite Mexican beer in the center. Fill the sides with a variety of fruits and snacks.

Top each can with chamoy (chile glaze) and a coat of Tajín. Drizzle more Tajín on top of fruit or leave it on the side for dipping. Drizzle a bit of Tapatio on top of the chicharrones right before serving.

Ingredient Note: Chamoy is a sweet and smoky chile glaze that can be drizzled on fruit or rimmed around a beer can or cocktail. Your taste buds will be dancing with the complex flavors of ancho chile peppers, lime juice, apricot jam, and sugar.

Entertaining Note: For your next fiesta, grab a box or large platter and create this epic Mexican beer box for the ultimate appetizer. I promise your friends will be floored when you bring out this over-the-top tray with authentic Mexican fixings. You should find everything you need to re-create this spread from your local Mexican market.

Crudité Platter with Green Goddess Dip

FOR THE GREEN GODDESS DIP

2 tablespoons fresh lemon juice

1 tablespoon olive oil

2 tablespoons chopped fresh flat-leaf parsley

1 cup fresh chopped leafy herbs of choice (such as chives, dill, tarragon, cilantro, and/or basil)

1 clove garlic, roughly chopped

1 cup full-fat Greek yogurt or sour cream

Sea salt and freshly ground black pepper

FOR SERVING

1 cup baby carrots

2 Persian cucumbers, sliced

1 bunch radishes, halved

1 cup cherry tomatoes, halved

¼ pound baby potatoes, parboiled

1 cup sugar snap peas

If you're planning a heavier meal with lots of meat and pasta, go for a lighter appetizer like a crudité platter. Serve an herbaceous fresh green goddess concoction alongside that doubles as an amazing salad dressing.

SERVES 4–6 AS AN APPETIZER

To make the green goddess dip, in a blender or a food processor, combine lemon juice, olive oil, parsley and other herbs, and garlic. Blend or pulse until smooth, about 30–60 seconds.

Transfer mixture to a serving bowl and stir in yogurt and ¼ teaspoon salt. Taste test for salt and pepper and adjust accordingly. Cover with plastic wrap and refrigerate until serving. (Green goddess dressing can be stored, tightly covered in the refrigerator, for 4–5 days.)

To serve, arrange baby carrots, cucumbers, radishes, cherry tomatoes, baby potatoes, and sugar snap peas on a platter or cheese board. Serve with green goddess dip.

Italian Melon & Mozzarella Cheese Board

1 ball (4 oz) burrata

Olive oil

Fresh basil leaves

Freshly ground black pepper

Mozzarella balls

Peaches, sliced

Tuscan yellow melon,
sliced and cut into triangles

Honeydew melon, sliced

Cantaloupe, sliced

Prosciutto

Fresh cherries

Marcona almonds

Crackers

When it comes to aperitifs, the Italians do them best. This cheese board was inspired by my trip to Italy, where the appetizers were almost as delicious as the meals (almost!). Serve up this Italian-style cheese board with one or a few Aperol Spritz variations (page 34) for a fun start to an Italian dinner party at home.

SERVES 4-6

In a small serving bowl, break open your ball of burrata cheese. Drizzle cheese with olive oil and sprinkle with fresh basil and pepper.

Arrange burrata bowl and mozzarella balls in 2 or 3 parts of the cheese board.

Fill the board with peach slices, yellow melon triangles, and honeydew slices.

Wrap cantaloupe slices with prosciutto and arrange on the board.

Fill small holes and crevices on the board with cherries, Marcona almonds, and crackers.

Cheese Plane

A cheese plane is used for cutting very thin slices of cheese and works great for semi- hard cheeses like Havarti, Gruyère, Monterey Jack, and Gouda.

Cheese Knives 101

Narrow Cheese Plane

A narrow cheese plane is a useful tool that can be used for a variety of semi-hard cheeses. Both sides are sharp, which is ideal for cutting into cheeses like Gouda, Muenster, and softer Cheddars.

Pronged or Soft- Cheese Knife

Use the prong-tipped end to cut into softer cheeses like Brie or Camembert. The long, slim blade usually has perforations to prevent sticking.

Parmesan Knife

A Parmesan knife is designed to contend with the hard texture of Parmesan cheese. Use the pointy end to score the cheese and the flat side to cut a wedge of cheese.

Spreader

Most of my cheese boards have a spreader. Its versatile design works well for softer cheeses like goat cheese, pimento cheese, or Boursin.

Chisel

A chisel knife is sharp on the edge for cutting cheese and wide for scooping and spreading. Ideally used for cheeses like Gorgonzola, Roquefort, and other creamy blues.

Mini Cleaver

A cleaver is great for cutting wedges, chunks, and thicker slices. The blade is a bit thicker and made for handling semi-hard cheeses like Cheddar or Pepper Jack.

Cheers!

Breakfast, lunch, dinner...happy hour. It really should have its own category, don't you think?! This chapter has a cocktail and bite for everyone and any occasion. It includes my tried-and-true batched margaritas that make an appearance at almost every party I host.

Bubbling Over

THE GOLDEN AGE OF SELTZER

You're not a true millennial unless you've spent a hot summer afternoon day drinking some hard seltzer. Much like wine coolers took the booze world by storm in the 80s (hello big shoulder pads and bigger drinks) and how Zima burst onto the scene in the early 90s, hard seltzer is truly seeing its golden age.

As trendy as it is, there is something for everyone. From organic kombucha hard seltzers to the fruit-flavored White Claw. The appeal, you might ask? Low in sugar, low in calories, low ABV, and extremely fruity and refreshing. Seltzers are made similarly to beer, but with a sugar base instead of barley that makes each sip 100 percent gluten free.

How to use? I'll forever make a batch of margaritas for any gathering, but I know that for a pool party or summer barbecue, a pack of hard seltzer is a must. Use it as a mixer for cocktails, blend with juice and fruit for a spritzer, or serve straight up ice cold for an effervescent and smooth beverage.

Blood Orange Margarita

Pink Himalayan salt

Sugar

1 blood orange or lime, for rim and garnish

2 fl oz silver (blanco) tequila

1 fl oz Cointreau or other orange liqueur

1 fl oz fresh lime juice

1 fl oz fresh blood orange juice

1–2 teaspoons agave nectar, or to taste

Being the marg lover that I am, this is my all-time favorite. If a drink could be a wing-woman, this would be mine—never too sweet, always perfect, easy to sip, and just the right amount of citrus. Served over crushed ice, with Himalayan salt on the rim, this blood orange margarita and its rich, ruby color is EVERYTHING.

MAKES 1 COCKTAIL

To salt glass rim, pour a light layer of pink Himalayan salt and sugar onto a small plate. Moisten a margarita glass rim with a blood orange or lime wedge. Dip glass in salt-sugar mix to coat rim evenly. Fill glass with crushed ice.

Fill a cocktail shaker with tequila, Cointreau, lime juice, blood orange juice, and agave (add more agave if you like your margs sweet!). Add ice, cover, shake vigorously for 10–15 seconds, and strain into prepared glass. Garnish with a fresh citrus slice.

Note: Grapefruit is a great option if you're not able to find blood oranges!

CBD Tincture & Tonic

2 fl oz gin

½ fl oz fresh lemon juice

10 mg CBD tincture

Tonic water, chilled

Marijuana leaves, for garnish (optional)

Lemon wedge, for garnish (optional)

Serving Tip: I love pairing this with something fresh like Citrus Shrimp with Avocado-Cilantro Crema (page 21) or the Farmers' Market Board (page 51) for happy hour.

Something new to try when you need something a little extra. This CBD gin and tonic is both familiar and edgy. Like the nice, cool kid at the party that you want to talk to but you're also kind of scared to say hi to. Trust me—there's no need to be intimidated. This elegant, refreshing cocktail only has four ingredients, so it's simple to make and even more satisfying to drink.

MAKES 1 COCKTAIL

Combine gin, lemon juice, and CBD tincture in a wineglass. Fill the glass with ice and top off with tonic water. Gently stir. Garnish glass with marijuana leaves and/or a lemon wedge, if using.

Poolside Watermelon Mojitos

FOR THE MINT SIMPLE SYRUP

1 cup sugar

1 cup water

1 handful mint leaves

FOR THE MOJITOS

2½ cups watermelon chunks

4 fl oz fresh lime juice

8 fl oz rum

3 tablespoons mint simple syrup

Fresh mint leaves, for serving

Watermelon chunks, for serving

Lime wheels, for serving

I don't know about you guys, but I am a HUGE watermelon lover. I can sit outside in the sun, eat a big wedge of watermelon, and be totally content. This drink satisfies that same subtly sweet, light, crisp craving and adds in an herbal, minty element as well. It's so quick and easy to make that you can add it to a drink menu, serve it by the glass, or make a big batch.

MAKES 2-4 COCKTAILS

To make the mint simple syrup, in a small saucepan over medium heat, combine sugar and water. Heat until sugar dissolves and mixture is clear. Remove from heat, add in a handful of fresh mint leaves (crush them with your hands to release their flavor), and let steep for 10–15 minutes. (The simple syrup can be stored in an airtight container for up to 3 weeks in the refrigerator.)

To make the mojitos, in a blender, combine watermelon chunks, fresh lime juice, rum, and simple syrup. Blend on high for 30 seconds, or until the mixture is smooth. Strain the mixture through a fine-mesh sieve and serve over ice. Garnish with fresh mint, watermelon chunks, and lime wheels.

French Onion Dip

2 tablespoons unsalted butter

2 medium yellow onions, finely chopped

3 cloves garlic, minced

2 teaspoons minced fresh rosemary

1½ cups sour cream

2 tablespoons chopped fresh chives + more for topping

¼ teaspoon cayenne pepper

Kosher salt and freshly ground black pepper

Ruffle chips, for serving

Within the first 10 minutes of being at Papa's house, I can usually count on two things: a chilled glass of pink champagne and a creamy bowl of French onion dip. My family jokes sometimes that you're not really a Van Lierde unless you like to consume copious amounts of French onion dip. It must be a Belgian thing. This dip is extremely creamy and deep with rich onion flavor. You'll never want store-bought again.

SERVES 4–5

In a medium sauté pan over medium heat, melt the butter. Once the butter has melted, add in onions and cook for 5 minutes, turning frequently. Reduce the heat to medium-low and cook for an additional 20–25 minutes, or until the onions are a deep golden brown. Add in garlic and cook for an additional 1–2 minutes.

Remove onion mixture from pan and let cool (you can speed this process up by putting it in the refrigerator).

In a medium bowl, mix together the cooled onion mixture, rosemary, sour cream, chives, cayenne, ½–1 teaspoon salt, and ½ teaspoon pepper. Taste test and add more salt or pepper if needed. Cover and refrigerate for at least 30 minutes or up to overnight to deepen the flavor. Serve with ruffle chips.

Cook's Tip: This dip can be made the morning of or the night before. Thaw out of the fridge for 10–15 minutes and stir together before serving.

Mediterranean Mule & Greek Meatball Bites

FOR THE MULE

1 fl oz fresh lime juice

2 fl oz vodka

1 fl oz limoncello

Ginger beer, chilled

FOR THE CUCUMBER-YOGURT SAUCE

1 cup Greek yogurt

½ cup grated cucumber

2 teaspoons minced fresh dill

1 tablespoon minced fresh flat-leaf parsley

1 garlic clove, minced

Juice of a small lemon

Kosher salt and freshly ground black pepper

FOR THE MEATBALLS

¼ onion, sliced

2 cloves garlic, roughly chopped

2 teaspoons fresh lemon juice

1 tablespoon olive oil + more for frying

¼ cup fresh flat-leaf parsley leaves

2 tablespoons minced fresh dill

1 teaspoon ground cumin

½ teaspoon dried red pepper flakes

Kosher salt and freshly ground black pepper

⅓ cup dried bread crumbs

1½ lb ground turkey

I can't tell you enough, I could eat these meatballs with a chilled, bright Mediterranean mule every single day. Each bite is like a juicy, herby flavor bomb topped with bright cucumber-yogurt sauce—YUM. Get ready to feel like you're having happy hour on a sunny balcony in the Mediterranean. All that's missing is the view!

MEDITERRANEAN MULE | MAKES 1 COCKTAIL

Squeeze lime juice into a copper cup or collins glass. Add in vodka and limoncello, and fill glass with ice. Stir mixture together and top off with ginger beer.

GREEK MEATBALL BITES | SERVES 4-6

To make the cucumber-yogurt sauce, in a small bowl, combine yogurt, grated cucumber, dill, parsley, garlic, lemon juice, 1½ teaspoons salt, and 1 teaspoon pepper. Taste test for seasoning and refrigerate until serving.

To make the meatballs, in a food processor, pulse together onion, garlic, lemon juice, olive oil, parsley, dill, cumin, red pepper flakes, ½ teaspoon salt, and ¼ teaspoon pepper until mixture is finely chopped. If you don't have a food processor, you can finely chop these ingredients together.

In a large bowl, mix together herb mixture, bread crumbs, and ground turkey. Divide mixture into 2-inch round meatballs.

Drizzle a large frying pan with olive oil and heat over medium-high heat. Cook meatballs in batches until golden brown on all sides and cooked through, about 5–7 minutes per batch. If the frying pan begins to look dry between batches, drizzle in a bit more oil.

Serve the meatballs with a little cucumber-yogurt sauce on a mini pita bread and top with fresh cucumber.

Note: Turn these into an easy meal by topping a pita with extra meatballs and fresh vegetables like tomato, cucumber, red onion, lettuce and crumbled feta cheese.

Green Chile Queso

2 tablespoons unsalted butter

¼ small yellow onion, finely diced

2 cloves garlic, minced

2 tablespoons all-purpose flour

1 cup milk

½ teaspoon kosher salt

½ teaspoon ground cumin

1 can (4.5 oz) green chiles

1 small jalapeño chile, seeded and minced

1 cup Monterey Jack cheese, shredded

1 cup Cheddar cheese, shredded

Hot sauce (optional)

Chopped fresh cilantro, for garnish

Tortilla chips, for serving

This green chile queso was just too good not to share with the masses. It's my most-requested side for taco nights, game days, or happy hours with friends. I will even make it as a pre-outing app with some salty, restaurant-worthy chips to snack on while I sip on a cocktail and get ready. The smooth, green chile–infused queso topped with a pinch of cilantro and a drizzle of hot sauce is just so, so good.

SERVES 4

In a small cast-iron or heavy-bottomed frying pan over medium heat, melt butter. Add in onion and sauté for 2–3 minutes, or until translucent. Add in garlic and continue to sauté for 1 minute. Sprinkle flour into pan and cook, stirring, for 1–2 minutes. Slowly whisk in milk. Whisk mixture continuously for 2–3 minutes, or until it begins to thicken, to make a roux.

Whisk salt, cumin, canned green chiles, and jalapeño into queso roux. Remove from heat and whisk in cheeses until they are melted and creamy.

Serve queso with a drizzle of hot sauce, if using, a sprinkling of freshly chopped cilantro, and tortilla chips alongside.

Note: To add heat, top with additional sliced jalapeño. For a mild version, leave out the jalapeños and omit the hot sauce.

Sparkling Spicy Paloma & Classic Guacamole

By now you've probably noticed I have a slight (okay, extreme) obsession with all things tequila. Aside from margaritas, these insanely refreshing, slightly sweetened palomas are at the top of the list. They have a little bit of spice and just enough sparkle in each sip. Serve them up with the PERFECT guacamole—it's such a balanced combo with all the right citrusy, spicy flavors!

FOR THE PALOMA

2 jalapeño chile slices

½ fl oz fresh lime juice

1 fl oz fresh grapefruit juice

2 fl oz silver (blanco) tequila

1 teaspoon agave nectar

Sparkling water

1 large grapefruit wedge, for garnish

Tajín (chile-lime seasoning salt)

FOR THE GUAC

4 ripe avocados

1½ tablespoons fresh lime juice (about 1 lime)

¼ red onion, finely diced

1 jalapeño chile, finely diced

½ teaspoon garlic powder

¼ cup chopped fresh cilantro

½–1 teaspoon kosher salt, or to taste

Tortilla chips or crudité vegetables, for serving

SPARKLING SPICY PALOMA | MAKES 1 COCKTAIL

Combine jalapeño slices, lime juice, grapefruit juice, tequila, and agave in a large glass. Muddle mixture together for 15–20 seconds. Fill the glass with ice and top with sparkling water. Mix together gently. Garnish cocktail with a grapefruit wedge dipped in chile-lime seasoning.

CLASSIC GUACAMOLE | SERVES 4–5

Slice avocados in half and remove the pits. With a large spoon, scoop out the avocado flesh and place in a medium mixing bowl.

Mash avocados with a fork until smooth but still slightly chunky and textured. Add in lime juice, red onion, jalapeño, garlic powder, chopped cilantro, and salt. Gently stir together until well combined.

Taste test for salt and seasoning, and serve immediately with chips or vegetables.

Modern Mai Tai

2 fl oz white rum

1 fl oz Cointreau or other orange liqueur

2 fl oz pineapple juice

½ fl oz fresh lime juice

1 teaspoon Luxardo maraschino cherry juice

1–2 drops almond extract

Pineapple wedge, for garnish

Pineapple leaf, for garnish

Luxardo maraschino cherries, for garnish

Mai Tai—the quintessential tropical cocktail that packs all of the vacation vibes into one rum-filled, slightly sweet glassful. Think of this as a modern makeover for that syrupy version at your local tiki bar. Fresh fruit juice, no added sugar, and beautiful garnishes make this a much-needed addition to your summer cocktail rotation!

MAKES 1 COCKTAIL

Fill a cocktail shaker with rum, Cointreau, pineapple juice, lime juice, maraschino cherry juice and almond extract. Fill the shaker with ice, cover, shake vigorously, and strain into a cocktail glass filled with ice.

Garnish with a pineapple wedge, pineapple leaf, and maraschino cherries.

Drink Cheat Sheet

You know your guests (and their drinking habits!) better than I do, but this easy guide should get you through any gathering, big or small, without anyone's drink running dry. I usually round up to the higher number, especially if it's a typical warm SoCal day.

Cocktails & Beverages	Wine	Water & Ice
A full bar is ambitious; narrow it down to 1 or 2 drinks that you'll serve for the night, or even a batched cocktail for something prepped and easy. Have a little club soda and juice like lemonade or pomegranate juice on hand for mocktails. 1–2 drinks per hour per person	Serving wine for a dinner party? There are roughly 4–5 glasses of wine in a bottle (4 if you take a big swig when you open it, like I do). I always plan for at least 1 bottle per person for a 3-hour dinner. Don't be afraid to buy an extra bottle or two if you think things will run longer. **Pro tip:** I always tell my friends to bring a bottle of wine when they ask if they can bring anything.	While they may seem boring, don't forget them! Always have a generous supply of ice and fresh water for self-serving.

Pink Negroni

2 fl oz gin

1 fl oz Campari

1 fl oz fresh grapefruit or blood orange juice

1–2 teaspoons simple syrup (see Cook's Tip)

Grapefruit zest strip, for garnish

Green olive, for garnish

I'm all about the occasional fancy, girly-girl drink and this one's pretty classic. With Campari, gin, and that citrus bite from the grapefruit juice, it goes well with both elevated dishes AND those super-easy snacks you have in the pantry. It's a refreshing hot summer day drink that'll make you feel like your backyard is an Italian courtyard.

MAKES 1 COCKTAIL

Fill a cocktail mixing glass or cocktail shaker with ice. Add gin, Campari, grapefruit juice, and simple syrup to taste. Stir mixture 15–20 times.

Place a large square ice cube in a lowball cocktail glass. Strain mixture into glass. Garnish with grapefruit peel and a green olive.

Cook's Tip: To make simple syrup, in a small saucepan over medium heat, combine equal parts sugar and water. Heat until sugar dissolves and mixture is clear. Store in a mason jar or other airtight container for up to a month in the refrigerator.

Pitcher Margaritas 3 Ways

CLASSIC MARGARITAS

1 (750 ml) bottle of your favorite tequila

1½ cups triple sec or other orange liqueur

1½ cups fresh lime juice + lime wedges

½–1 cup agave nectar (see Note)

Kosher salt

It's no secret that I love a margarita, but these are one of those cocktails that when you get to the last sip you just KNOW that you're going to make another batch. They're extremely addicting and incredibly smooth. I make all three versions on the regular and friends always expect a jug of margs if I'm hosting. The best part: they come together in just five minutes (seriously!). Go with the pomegranate for something sweet, the pineapple for something funky, and the classic for...well, you know!

MAKES 8–10 MARGARITAS PER PITCHER

To make classic margaritas, in a large pitcher, combine tequila, triple sec, lime juice, and agave nectar to taste, and stir well. Chill margarita batches for 1–2 hours before serving, or simply fill glasses with crushed ice and serve at once.

To salt glass rims, pour a light layer of kosher salt onto a small plate. Moisten margarita glass rims with a lime wedge and dip glasses in salt to coat rim evenly.

PINEAPPLE MEZCAL MARGARITAS: Sub tequila with mezcal and add 1 cup pineapple juice.

POMEGRANATE MARGARITAS: Add in 1 cup pomegranate juice.

Note: Start with ½ cup of agave nectar, taste test, and add more to your liking. Like your margaritas on the tart side? Just leave out the agave, or add less.

Pimento Cheese Dip

4 oz cream cheese, at room temp

⅓ cup mayonnaise

2 cups freshly shredded sharp Cheddar cheese (not pre-shredded)

4 oz pimento peppers, drained and chopped

1 teaspoon Worcestershire sauce

½ teaspoon garlic powder

½ teaspoon onion powder

Salt and freshly ground black pepper

½ teaspoon cayenne pepper

Crackers, for serving

Crudité veggies, for serving

I may be West Coast through and through, but I am all about this Southern staple. If you've never had pimento cheese, get ready to meet your new obsession. This cheesy, smoky, easy-to-make goodness is so versatile and undoubtedly delicious. Serve with crackers, pretzels, and veggies, or use this creamy spread as a topping for burger night.

SERVES 4–5

In a medium bowl, beat together cream cheese and mayo until fluffy and creamy.

Add in sharp Cheddar cheese, pimento peppers, Worcestershire sauce, garlic powder, onion powder, black pepper to taste, and cayenne pepper. Beat mixture together until the mixture is thoroughly combined.

Taste test for black pepper and cayenne, and add salt if needed.

Transfer mixture to a serving bowl and serve right away with crackers or crudité, or let flavors marry for 20–30 minutes. The longer the flavors marinate, the stronger the dip's flavor.

Note: Dip can be made ahead of time and stored in the refrigerator for up to a week. Be sure to bring to room temperature and stir before serving.

Poke Nachos

FOR THE POKE

½ lb sushi-grade albacore or ahi tuna

2 tablespoons soy sauce

Juice of 1 lime

FOR THE MANGO-CUCUMBER PICO

1 mango cheek, diced

½ small cucumber, diced

¼ cup red onion, finely diced

½ jalapeño chile, seeded and finely diced

1 handful fresh cilantro, chopped

FOR THE SPICY MAYO

½ cup mayonnaise

2 tablespoons sriracha sauce

FOR THE WONTON CHIPS

Canola or vegetable oil, for frying

20–25 wonton wrappers, halved or quartered

½ avocado, finely diced

¼ cup thinly sliced radishes

1 tablespoon sesame seeds

Lime wedges, for serving (optional)

My mouth starts watering every time I even mention poke nachos. Layers of raw tuna and sweet and savory mango pico on top of crispy wonton chips topped with creamy diced avocado, radish slices, and sesame seeds—it's visually STUNNING and packed with all the best flavors.

SERVES 3-4

To make the poke, cut tuna into ½-inch dice. In a medium bowl, mix tuna with soy sauce and lime juice. Set aside.

To make the pico, in a small bowl, mix together mango, cucumber, red onion, jalapeño, and cilantro until combined.

To make the spicy mayo, in a separate small bowl, whisk together mayonnaise and sriracha until combined. Transfer to a squeeze bottle or lock-top bag and set aside.

To make the wonton chips, in a medium cast-iron frying pan over medium heat, heat 1 inch of oil until a deep-frying thermometer registers 350°F. Line a plate with paper towels. Fry a few wonton wrappers at a time for about 15 seconds on each side. Remove wontons to paper towel–lined plate to drain.

Arrange wonton chips on a baking sheet or serving platter. Top chips evenly with poke mixture and mango pico. Using the squeeze bottle or the lock-top bag with the corner snipped off, drizzle spicy mayonnaise evenly over nachos. Top with diced avocado, radish slices, and sesame seeds. Serve with extra lime wedges, if using.

Cook's Tips: You can use store-bought wonton chips or even tortilla chips if you're in a time crunch. And, you can always swap out the tuna for salmon if you like. Just make sure it's sushi-grade for eating raw.

Strawberry Peach Frosé with Prosciutto & Melon Bites

1 bottle (750 ml) of your favorite rosé

FOR THE STRAWBERRY SIMPLE SYRUP

1 cup granulated sugar

1 cup water

2 cups strawberries, quartered

FOR THE STRAWBERRY-PEACH FROSÉ

2 cups frozen peach slices

Strawberry simple syrup, to taste

¼ cup limoncello

¼ cup vodka

FOR THE PROSCIUTTO & MELON BITES

½ ripe cantaloupe

3 oz prosciutto

Let me introduce you to my best gal Katie. She's such a big part of this cookbook, and this recipe is an ode to her bachelorette weekend in Charleston one fine summer. Seriously, nothing tops a resort-style pool, your closest friends, and the perfect, refreshing drink to sip on all day. The sweet, salty prosciutto and melon combo paired with this strawberry peach frosé is perfect for snacking poolside or at a summer cocktail party alfresco.

STRAWBERRY-PEACH FROSÉ | MAKES 4 DRINKS

Pour your bottle of rosé into ice cube molds and freeze for at least 4–6 hours or up to overnight. The wine will not freeze solid, but will help keep the drink frozen.

To make the strawberry simple syrup, in a small saucepan over medium heat, heat sugar and water until sugar dissolves and mixture is clear. Add in strawberries and bring to a gentle simmer. Transfer syrup to a separate bowl to cool and allow strawberries to steep for 30 minutes.

Strain syrup from strawberries into a jar. Before using, refrigerate syrup for at least 30–60 minutes, or overnight. You can fast-track this by putting it in the freezer, too.

In a blender, combine frozen rosé blocks, frozen peach slices, strawberry simple syrup (start with ⅓ cup, adding more to taste), limoncello, vodka, and 1 cup ice. Blend for 30 seconds, or until smooth and frothy.

PROSCIUTTO & MELON BITES | SERVES 4

Slice cantaloupe into long wedges and cut away rind. Wrap a piece of prosciutto tightly around each chunk of melon. Arrange on a serving platter and serve right away, or chilled.

Cook's Tip: Consider this a PSA to freeze your wine and peaches and make the delicious strawberry simple syrup the night before. This way you're whipping up drinks poolside in 10 minutes flat.

Blend just enough until the batch is smooth—overblending will cause the mixture to melt faster.

Shishito Peppers with "The Sauce"

FOR "THE SAUCE"

½ cup mayonnaise

¼ cup ketchup

½ teaspoon Worcestershire sauce

½ teaspoon freshly ground black pepper

1 teaspoon garlic powder

1 teaspoon Old Bay or Cajun seasoning

½ teaspoon cayenne pepper

FOR THE PEPPERS

3 cups shishito peppers

1 tablespoon olive oil

1 lemon (optional)

Flaky sea salt and freshly ground black pepper

Shishito peppers have made a name for themselves at trendy restaurants, but they are also a dish that is SO easily prepared at home. These flavorful peppers are charred and served alongside "The Sauce." Anytime I serve a batch of this creamy, Cajun-style aioli to friends, I always get asked, "Is that *the* sauce?!" It's made quite a name for itself, and for good reason. It's oozing with spicy flavors and makes the perfect pair for charred vegetables (or, try it with fries).

SERVES 4

To make "The Sauce," in a small bowl, whisk together mayonnaise, ketchup, Worcestershire sauce, black pepper, garlic powder, Old Bay seasoning, and cayenne until well combined. Cover and refrigerate for at least ½ hour before serving to let the flavors come together.

Meanwhile, prepare the peppers. Rinse the shishito peppers and pat dry completely with a clean dish towel or with paper towels. In a large bowl, drizzle olive oil all over peppers, toss until they are well coated, and set aside.

Heat a medium, heavy-bottomed frying pan over medium heat for 1–2 minutes. Add in one pepper to test if the pan is hot enough: it should sizzle on contact. Add in remaining peppers and cook for 1 minute on each side, allowing each pepper to char, about 8–10 minutes total.

Transfer peppers to a serving platter and juice half a lemon over the peppers if desired. Sprinkle generously with flaky sea salt and black pepper, and serve with dipping sauce.

Cozy Night In

I'm all about taking my restaurant favorites and turning them into staples to make at home any night of the week. Everything from takeout pad thai and fish tacos to ramen: I think we've covered all the bases for an epic cozy night in.

Green Suiza Chicken Enchiladas

FOR THE CHICKEN

2 teaspoons cumin

1 teaspoon ground chili powder

1 teaspoon dried oregano

1 teaspoon garlic powder

Kosher salt and freshly ground black pepper

3 boneless, skinless chicken breast halves

3 tablespoons olive oil

½ yellow onion, diced

1 can (4.5 oz) green chiles

Juice of ½ lime

1 cup chicken stock

1 cup light beer (pale ale or lager)

FOR THE ENCHILADA SAUCE

10 tomatillos, husked and rinsed

½ yellow onion, chopped

1–2 jalapeño chiles, seeded for less spice

1 teaspoon ground cumin

1 teaspoon garlic powder

1 handful fresh cilantro leaves

Juice of ½ lime

½ cup chicken stock

FOR THE ENCHILADAS

8–10 medium corn tortillas

1–2 cups shredded Monterey Jack cheese

Sour cream, for garnish

Chopped fresh cilantro, for garnish

Sliced jalapeño chiles, for garnish (seeded for less spice)

Sliced avocado, for garnish

In college, one of the first things I taught myself how to cook was a damn good platter of enchiladas. I could feed a ton of people with few ingredients. Each enchilada is filled with chicken that's been slow-simmered with green chiles and beer and topped with a bright, rich tomatillo sauce. Add these to your next fiesta or weekend dinner rotation.

SERVES 4–5

In a small bowl, stir together cumin, chili powder, oregano, garlic powder, 1 teaspoon salt, and ½ teaspoon pepper. Season chicken generously with the spice mix.

In a large Dutch oven over medium heat, drizzle the olive oil and sauté onion for 3–4 minutes, until translucent. Using a slotted spoon, remove onion and set aside in a separate bowl.

Add chicken to the pan and sear on each side for 3 minutes—chicken will cook through during the full braise. Return onions to pan and add green chiles, lime juice, chicken stock, and beer. Make sure chicken is covered halfway with beer and stock. Gently stir and bring to a simmer, reduce heat to medium-low, cover, and cook for 30–40 minutes. Remove chicken and shred with two forks. Return chicken back to braising liquid and toss well.

To make the enchilada sauce, preheat oven to 400°F. Spread tomatillos, jalapeños, and onion on a rimmed baking sheet. Drizzle with olive oil and rub each ingredient to coat with oil. Roast for 15–20 minutes, or until tomatillos are tender and golden (this can be done while chicken is braising).

In a blender or Vitamix, blend together roasted tomatillos, onion, jalapeño (taste test before adding the second), 1 teaspoon salt, cumin, garlic powder, cilantro, lime juice, and chicken stock and blend until smooth. Taste test for salt and spice once blended, and adjust accordingly.

Lower oven temperature to 350°F. Pour ½ cup of enchilada sauce into the bottom of a medium casserole dish. Make a small assembly station of sauce, tortillas, cheese, and chicken. Dip each tortilla lightly into sauce and fill with a small handful of cheese and ¼–½ cup shredded chicken. Roll each tortilla and arrange in the baking dish. Top enchiladas with remaining sauce and an even layer of shredded cheese.

Bake for 15–20 minutes, or until cheese is browned and melted on top. Top off baked enchiladas with a dollop of sour cream, and a garnishing of chopped cilantro, sliced jalapeños, and sliced avocado.

The Best BBQ Chicken Nachos

8 oz tortilla chips (a little less than a standard bag)

2 cups freshly shredded sharp Cheddar cheese

1 cup black beans, drained and rinsed

½ lb cooked chicken breasts (rotisserie is okay), skin removed and meat shredded

1 cup of BBQ sauce + more for topping

½ avocado, diced

¼ red onion, finely diced

¼ cup chopped green onions

¼ cup chopped fresh cilantro

1 jalapeño chile, thinly sliced

Sour cream, for topping

One of my secret weapon recipes. No big game day is complete without these simple yet super flavorful bbq chicken nachos. This is that recipe that my friends text me for on Sunday morning of the Super Bowl. This thick platter of nachos is baked with juicy pulled bbq chicken, beans, and melty cheddar cheese. Then topped with an array of fresh toppings like cilantro, jalapeños, onions, avocado and more bbq sauce. I never serve them without a huge dollop of sour cream, my favorite.

SERVES 4-6

Preheat oven to 425°F.

On a rimmed baking sheet, arrange the tortilla chips in an even layer. Top chips with Cheddar cheese and black beans.

In a medium bowl, mix together shredded chicken breast and 1 cup of your favorite BBQ sauce until the chicken is evenly coated. Top chips with BBQ chicken and bake for 10–15 minutes, or until the cheese is bubbling.

Drizzle a bit more BBQ sauce on top of nachos. Garnish nachos with avocado, red onion, green onions, cilantro, and jalapeño. Top with sour cream in 4–5 dollops and serve right away.

Cook's Tip: These are just as delicious vegetarian. Skip the chicken and use canned, shredded jackfruit for a veggie friendly option.

Cheddar & Chive Corn Bread with Honey Butter

FOR THE CORN BREAD

⅓ cup butter, melted + more for pan

1 cup stone-ground cornmeal

1 cup all-purpose flour

¼ cup sugar

4 teaspoons baking powder

2 large eggs

1 cup milk

2 tablespoons honey

1 cup shredded sharp Cheddar cheese

3 tablespoons minced chives

FOR THE HONEY BUTTER

½ cup (1 stick) unsalted butter, softened

¼ cup honey

Pinch of salt

No bowl of chili is complete without a delicious hunk of corn bread. This sweet and moist loaf is laced with cheddar cheese and chives and topped with a rich honey butter that you'll want to smother each slice with.

MAKES 9 PIECES

Preheat oven to 400°F. Grease an 8 x 8-inch square baking pan with butter and set aside.

In a large bowl, whisk together cornmeal, all-purpose flour, sugar, and baking powder and set aside.

In a separate bowl, mix together eggs, milk, melted butter, and honey. Gently stir the wet ingredients into the dry ingredients until just combined; do not overmix.

Gently fold in the Cheddar cheese and chives. Pour batter into prepared baking pan and bake for 18–20 minutes, or until top is golden and a toothpick inserted in the center of the bread comes out clean. Let bread cool for 10 minutes before serving.

While the corn bread is baking, prepare the honey butter. Add the butter to the bowl of a stand mixer (or use a hand mixer). Beat the butter until light and fluffy. Pour in the honey and a pinch of salt and continue mixing until the mixture is smooth and creamy. Transfer the honey butter to a bowl or jar for serving.

Sunday Chipotle Chorizo Chili

2 tablespoons olive oil

1 yellow onion, diced

1 red bell pepper, diced

6 cloves garlic, chopped

3 tablespoons tomato paste

2–3 chipotle chiles in adobo, roughly chopped + 1½ tablespoons chile liquid

2 tablespoons ground cumin

2 tablespoons chili powder

2 teaspoons dried oregano

Kosher salt and freshly ground black pepper

6 oz pork chorizo

1 lb ground turkey

6 oz light beer (pale ale or lager works great)

2 cans (14 oz each) diced fire-roasted tomatoes with juices

2 cans (16 oz each) pinto or black beans

TOPPINGS

Fritos

Fresh cilantro

Shredded Cheddar cheese

Sour cream

An easy, classic chili recipe with a modern revival. Chili always has a secret ingredient or two, and this one's are chorizo and beer. The chorizo adds extra spice, flavor, and richness that can't be beat. The beer adds savory notes and aromas with every bite. This chili is downright perfect and a menu must for any cozy Sunday. Be sure to serve alongside Cheddar & Chive Corn Bread (opposite) and plenty of Fritos.

SERVES 6–8

In a large Dutch oven over medium-high heat, combine olive oil and onion, bell pepper, and garlic. Sauté for 5–6 minutes, or until the onion has softened and is fragrant.

Stir in the tomato paste, chipotle chiles and chile liquid, cumin, chili powder, oregano, and a sprinkling of salt and pepper. Cook for 1–2 minutes.

Add in the pork chorizo and ground turkey, breaking them up with a wooden spoon. Sprinkle evenly with salt and pepper and brown meat for 8–10 minutes, or until turkey is cooked through.

Add in beer and simmer until the liquid has reduced, about 4–5 minutes.

Add in the fire-roasted tomatoes with their juices and beans. Bring mixture to a low simmer, partially cover, and cook, stirring occasionally, until liquid has thickened and become very flavorful, at least 30–45 minutes, but ideally 1–2 hours to deepen the flavors. If chili has thickened too much, use a bit of water or broth to thin it out to your desired consistency.

To serve, ladle chili into individual serving bowls and top with Fritos, cilantro, cheese, and sour cream.

Juicy Citrus Carnitas

4 lb pork shoulder roast

3 teaspoons kosher salt

3 teaspoons cumin

3 teaspoons chili powder

2 teaspoons dried oregano

5 cloves garlic

2 yellow onions, peeled and quartered

1 jalapeño chile, chopped

Juice of 2 oranges

Juice of 2 limes

1 bottle (12 oz) good light beer (I use Modelo)

1 cup chicken stock

1 tablespoon olive oil (if needed)

FOR SERVING

Corn tortillas

Crumbled cotija cheese

Chopped fresh cilantro

Quick-Pickled Red Onions (below)

Guacamole (page 81)

Green Tomatillo Salsa (page 222)

The perfect meal to make when you've got people coming over, but don't feel like cooking. Throw a pork shoulder into a slow cooker with a bunch of spices, salt, beer, and fresh citrus juices. In 6 to 8 hours, you'll have unbelievably tender carnitas, perfect for tacos, bowls, or tostadas.

SERVES 6

Place pork shoulder roast in a slow cooker. Rub with salt, cumin, chili powder, and dried oregano. Add in garlic cloves, onions, jalapeño, orange juice, lime juice, beer and chicken stock.

Cover slow cooker and cook on low for 8 hours or on high for 5–6 hours.

Using two forks, shred meat directly in the slow cooker. or remove to a cutting board and shred.

To crisp up the carnitas, preheat broiler. Spread shredded carnitas evenly on a rimmed baking sheet and drizzle with liquid from the slow cooker. Broil meat for 5–10 minutes, or until the edges start to turn golden and crispy. Alternatively, meat can be browned in a frying pan on the stove top. Drizzle pan with 1 tablespoon of olive oil and add carnitas, spread evenly, and drizzle slow-cooker liquid over meat. Cook over medium-high heat until the liquid has mostly evaporated and the meat starts to become crispy and golden on the edges.

To assemble, top the corn tortillas with meat. Serve with cheese, cilantro, pickled red onions, guac, and salsa.

QUICK-PICKLED RED ONIONS

Thinly slice 1 red onion and place in a large jar or airtight container. Pour in ¾ cup apple cider vinegar, 1 tablespoon sugar or honey, and ½ teaspoon kosher salt. Shake jar vigorously and place in the refrigerator for 1 hour. Shake the jar up every 15 minutes or so for a faster pickle.

Will keep for up to 2 weeks in the refrigerator.

IPA Beer-Battered Fish Tacos

FOR THE CHIPOTLE MAYO

1 cup mayonnaise

Zest and juice of 1 lime

1 teaspoon garlic powder

1 tablespoon canned chile in adobo, liquid only

FOR THE PICKLED SLAW

3 cups shredded cabbage or packaged coleslaw mix

½ cup fresh cilantro, chopped

1 jalapeño chile, seeded and thinly sliced

2 tablespoons honey

Juice of 1 lime

1 tablespoon red wine vinegar

¼ teaspoon kosher salt

FOR THE FISH TACOS

Grapeseed or vegetable oil, for frying

1½ cups all-purpose flour

1½ teaspoons ground cumin

1½ teaspoons garlic powder

1 teaspoon chili powder

½ teaspoon cayenne pepper

1 bottle golden beer (such as IPA or lager)

2 lb skinless cod or halibut fillets, cut into 3-inch by 1-inch pieces

Kosher salt

Corn or flour tortillas, warmed

1 cup crumbled cotija cheese

½ cup thinly sliced radishes

Hot sauce, for serving

My fav local taco place, Pour Vida, serves up the most epic taco menu. I could probably eat their beer-battered fish taco seven out of seven days a week and be happy, it's that good. I went on a personal taco quest to recreate this tortilla-wrapped magic, and I think I have finally achieved the most crispy, fresh, and flavorful fish taco known to man (or Southern California). Fried to golden beer-battered perfection and topped with a zesty slaw mixture and a creamy chipotle sauce. Serve with an ice-cold beer or a blood orange marg (page 70).

SERVES 4–6

To make the chipotle mayo, whisk together mayonnaise, lime zest and juice, garlic powder, and chipotle in adobo liquid until smooth and creamy. Set aside.

To make the pickled slaw, in a medium bowl, mix together cabbage, cilantro, jalapeño, honey, lime juice, vinegar, and salt. Toss together until fully mixed, cover, and refrigerate until serving.

To prepare the tacos, in a large Dutch oven, heat 2 inches of oil over medium-high heat until a deep-frying thermometer registers 360°F. Line a plate with paper towels and set aside.

In a large bowl, whisk together flour, cumin, garlic powder, chili powder, and cayenne until combined. Pour in bottle of beer and whisk together until just combined. Do not let batter sit out; best if used right away.

Working in batches of four, coat each fish piece in the beer batter. Fry for about 3–4 minutes per batch, or until cooked through and golden brown. Drain fish on paper towel–lined plate and sprinkle with salt immediately after frying. Be careful not to overcrowd your oil, and let oil return to 360° between batches. Repeat until all the fish is fried.

Spread an even layer of chipotle mayo onto each tortilla and top with a piece of fish, pickled slaw, crumbled cheese, radishes, and hot sauce of choice.

Vegetarian Ramen

2 teaspoons sesame oil

4 cloves garlic, minced

1 tablespoon minced fresh ginger

1 cup sliced shiitake mushroom caps

3 green onions, thinly sliced

½ cup grated carrots

6 cups vegetable stock

1 tablespoon unsalted butter

3–4 tablespoons soy sauce

2 tablespoons sambal oelek chile paste

½ teaspoon sriracha sauce

2 dried ramen bricks (discard seasoning packets)

2 heads baby bok choy, trimmed and halved

Sesame seeds, for topping (optional)

This Japanese-inspired vegetarian ramen is an extremely simplified version of the classic. This cozy-night-in staple can be made in under a half an hour. Filled with tons of fresh veggies (use whatever you have!) swimming in a rich garlic and ginger broth and tender ramen noodles, I promise you'll be slurping every last drop.

SERVES 2

In a large Dutch oven or stockpot over medium heat, heat sesame oil.

Add in garlic and ginger and cook for about a minute, or until fragrant. Add in shiitake mushrooms, half of the green onions, and carrots and cook for 3-4 minutes.

Add in stock, butter, soy sauce, sambal oelek, and sriracha. Bring to a slow simmer. Taste test broth and add in more soy sauce or sriracha to your liking.

Stir dried ramen bricks (sans seasoning) into simmering stock and cook for 2-3 minutes. Add in bok choy and cook for 1-2 additional minutes, stirring everything together.

Divide soup among shallow bowls and top with a bit of extra broth. Top with remaining green onions and, if desired, and sprinkle with sesame seeds.

Personalized Pad Thai

8 oz rice noodles

FOR THE PAD THAI

2 tablespoons oil (high-heat oil like vegetable or avocado)

1 red bell pepper, halved and thinly sliced crosswise

3 cloves garlic, minced

Protein of choice*

Kosher salt and freshly ground black pepper

2 eggs, lightly whisked

1 cup bean sprouts

FOR THE SAUCE

¼ cup soy sauce

¼ cup brown sugar

2 tablespoons rice vinegar

1 tablespoon fresh lime juice

1 tablespoon fish sauce

1–2 teaspoons crushed red pepper flakes

TOPPINGS

½ cup peanuts, chopped

¼ cup chopped fresh cilantro

3 green onions, thinly sliced

Note: Alternatively, omit the scrambled eggs and garnish each serving with a fried egg. In a small nonstick skillet, heat 1 tablespoon oil or butter over medium heat. Crack an egg into the pan and cook until the white is completely set. Serve atop pad thai.

Whenever I visit my parents, we almost always grab Thai food from their local joint, Thippawan. We all order pad thai, all with our own special touches. This restaurant-style classic can be made even better at home. Swap in any of your favorite proteins and be sure to serve it up with plenty of toppings like cilantro, peanuts, green onions, and—if you're like my family—a drippy fried egg.

SERVES 4

*SHRIMP: 1 lb, peeled and deveined | Cooking time: 1–2 minutes a side

*CHICKEN: 1 lb breast meat, thinly sliced | Cooking time: 3–4 minutes a side

*BEEF: 1 lb skirt steak, very thinly sliced across the grain, 2-inch pieces | Cooking time: 1–2 minutes a side

*TOFU: 8 oz firm tofu, patted dry and cut into ¾-inch pieces, sprinkled with cornstarch | Cooking time: 1–2 minutes a side

Cook rice noodles according to package instructions. (The rule of thumb is to place noodles into a shallow bowl and add enough boiling water to cover them. Let noodles sit for 7–8 minutes, or until tender, and drain.)

To make the pad thai, in a large wok or nonstick pan over medium-high heat, heat oil. Add in bell pepper and cook for 3–4 minutes. Stir in garlic and cook for an additional minute, or until fragrant. Add in protein of choice and sprinkle with salt and black pepper. Cooking according to protein time given above.

To make the sauce, in a small bowl, whisk together soy sauce, brown sugar, rice vinegar, lime juice, fish sauce, and red pepper flakes. Set aside.

Push the veggies and protein to one side of the pan and pour in the eggs. Scramble eggs until just set, then mix in with the protein-vegetable mixture.

Add in the bean sprouts, sauce mixture, and noodles. Toss everything together until coated. Cook for an additional 3–4 minutes, tossing frequently, until the sauce has thickened up a bit.

Serve with small bowls of chopped peanuts, cilantro, and green onions for topping.

Chile-Garlic Edamame

1 lb frozen edamame in shells

1 teaspoon sesame oil

1 tablespoon olive oil

1 tablespoon low-sodium
soy sauce

1 tablespoon sweet red
chile sauce

Juice of ½ lime

1 teaspoon crushed red
pepper flakes

3 cloves garlic, minced

2 teaspoons minced fresh ginger

These chile-garlic soybeans are the perfect snack alongside a cold Sapporo or cup of your favorite sake. They're spicy, rich in garlic flavor, and highly addicting. Serve this up in ten minutes or less while you bide your time before dinner.

SERVES 3–4

Cook edamame according to package instructions, and set aside.

In a small bowl, whisk together sesame oil, olive oil, soy sauce, red chile sauce, lime juice, red pepper flakes, garlic, and ginger.

Heat a medium sauté pan over medium heat. Add in sauce mixture and heat for 1–2 minutes. Add in edamame and stir mixture together. Cook for an additional 3–5 minutes, or until edamame have warmed through and the sauce has thickened a bit.

Transfer edamame to a serving bowl and serve right away with another empty bowl for shells.

Miso Soup

4 cups vegetable or dashi broth

3–4 tablespoons white
miso paste

1 small head lacinato (Tuscan)
kale, chopped

1 bunch of green onions,
thinly sliced

¼ cup cubed firm tofu

Salt, as needed

I have a strange and unshakable love for miso soup. I simply cannot have sushi without it. I love how satisfied I feel after something so light and delicate. Made with just five ingredients, this miso soup is ready in twenty minutes. Serve piping hot alongside your favorite sushi.

SERVES 4

Put vegetable or dashi broth in a medium pot over medium-high heat and bring to a low simmer.

In a small bowl, combine miso paste and ½ cup of warm broth. Whisk together until smooth. Stir this into the broth on the stove; this will ensure a smooth soup texture.

Add kale, green onions, and tofu to the soup and simmer on low for five minutes. Stir together once more before serving and taste test, adding more miso paste or salt if needed. Serve warm with large soup spoons.

No shame in my entertaining takeout game. Sushi is something I LOVE to order in. I'm not trying to level up to my sushi chef from my fav local spot, so instead I add a few homemade sides like miso soup and chile-garlic edamame to our usual takeout order. This is perfect when you have just a few people coming over. Set up everything on your coffee table with a few bottles of sake, turn on some great music, and have a casual, tasty night in.

Date Night at Home

There is absolutely nothing wrong with throwing on your sexiest lounge set and staying in. While I love going out on the town for a romantic meal, there is something so intimate about turning on your favorite playlist and lighting a few candles while you make that special someone in your life a meal they'll never forget.

Mezcal-Marinated Steak Fajitas

⅓ cup fresh lime juice

⅓ cup fresh orange juice

½ cup mezcal or tequila

3 tablespoons soy sauce

4 tablespoons olive oil (divided)

½ cup chopped fresh cilantro
+ more for serving

2 tablespoons canned chipotle
chile liquid (more if you like
it spicy)

3 cloves garlic, minced

1 tablespoon brown sugar

2 teaspoons chili powder

1 teaspoon ground cumin

1 teaspoon paprika

1½ lb skirt steak

2 bell peppers (color of your
choice), sliced into ¼-inch-
thick strips

½ white onion, thinly sliced

Kosher salt and freshly ground
black pepper

FOR SERVING

Corn or flour tortillas

Classic Guacamole (page 81)

Pico de gallo salsa

Sour cream

If you're looking for a casual date night where you can still turn up the heat, head to the grill. One of my favorite ways to spice up dinner at home is to simply take things outside. Light a few candles on your patio or balcony and grill up these fiery mezcal-marinated steak fajitas. Tender skirt steak marinated in a rich mezcal-citrus blend, charred to perfection, and served alongside all of the classic fajita accoutrements. Be sure to pair with a tart blood orange margarita (page 70)!

SERVES 4

In a small bowl, whisk together lime juice, orange juice, mezcal, soy sauce, 2 tablespoons olive oil, cilantro, chile liquid, garlic, brown sugar, chili powder, cumin, and paprika. In a large bowl, pour marinade over steak, making sure steak is submerged, or combine steak and marinade in a large lock-top bag. Allow steak to marinate for at least 4 hours or up to overnight.

Prepare a charcoal or gas grill for direct grilling over medium-high heat, or heat a cast-iron grill pan over medium-high heat on the stove top. Grill steak for 2–3 minutes on each side (for medium-rare), or until charred. Transfer steak to a cutting board, tent with foil, and let rest for 10 minutes. Slice across the grain into ½-inch-thick strips about 2 inches long.

Heat a large, heavy-bottomed frying pan over medium-high heat. Add in remaining 2 tablespoons olive oil, bell peppers, onion, 1 teaspoon salt, and a few turns of the pepper mill. Sauté for about 8–10 minutes, or until peppers are slightly tender and their skin is charred.

To serve, char corn or flour tortillas over medium-high heat on a grill, gas flame, or in a dry frying pan for 15–20 seconds on each side. Keep tortillas warm in a dishcloth dampened with warm water.

Arrange steak, peppers, and charred tortillas on a serving platter with bowls of guacamole, pico de gallo, and sour cream.

Lasagna with Béchamel

FOR THE MEAT SAUCE

1 tablespoon olive oil

1 medium yellow onion, diced

4 cloves garlic, minced

2 teaspoons dried oregano

2 lb ground beef

Salt and freshly ground
black pepper

2 jars (24 oz each) of your
favorite marinara sauce

FOR THE BÉCHAMEL
SAUCE

4 tablespoons unsalted butter

¼ cup all-purpose flour

3½ cups milk, warmed

Pinch of nutmeg

1 cup freshly shredded
Parmesan cheese

FOR THE LASAGNA

16 oz lasagna noodles (fresh
or dried)

16 oz low-moisture mozzarella
cheese, freshly shredded

Chopped fresh flat-leaf parsley,
for garnish

Make it a double! Date night, that is. Double dates are inevitable and while I usually love them, if I'm in the mood to feel extra comfortable, I always ditch the restaurant and invite everyone over. For a dish that is truly restaurant-quality at home, it's this lasagna. This classic is made a bit richer and more decadent with a few creamy béchamel layers. Once you make lasagna like this, you'll never go back!

SERVES 6–8

To make the meat sauce, in a large pot or Dutch oven over medium heat, heat olive oil. Add in onion and cook for 8–10 minutes, or until onion is soft and translucent. Add in garlic and oregano and cook for 1–2 minutes, or until fragrant. Add in ground beef. Using a wooden spoon, begin to break up the beef. Sprinkle evenly with salt and pepper and cook for 7–8 minutes, or until the meat has browned.

Add 2 jars marinara sauce to the meat mixture and stir together. Bring mixture to a low simmer and turn heat down to low. Cover and cook for 15–20 minutes.

To make the béchamel sauce, in a large saucepan over medium heat, melt butter. When butter is melted, whisk in flour. Cook, whisking constantly, for 1–2 minutes, or until golden. Slowly whisk in the milk, 1 cup at a time, whisking after each addition until mixture is smooth and no lumps remain.

Cook béchamel sauce for 5–6 minutes, or until the sauce is creamy and thick enough to coat the back of a wooden spoon. Remove from heat and add in nutmeg and shredded Parmesan cheese. Taste test for salt and pepper and season accordingly.

Preheat oven to 350°F.

To assemble the lasagna, in a deep 9 x 13-inch baking dish or roasting pan, spread 1 cup of meat marinara mixture on the bottom of the dish. Layer in an even layer of lasagna noodles. Layer in another 1–2 cups of meat sauce or enough to evenly coat the lasagna noodles. Add in 1 cup of the white sauce in an even layer on top of marinara and sprinkle evenly with shredded mozzarella cheese. Repeat layers, reserving ½–1 cup of shredded mozzarella cheese.

Pour the remaining meat sauce and white sauce over the last layer of lasagna noodles and top with remaining mozzarella cheese. Bake for 30–40 minutes, or until top is golden and bubbling. Let stand for 10–15 minutes after baking and garnish with fresh parsley before serving.

Bacon & Mozzarella-Stuffed Meatball Sandwiches

8 oz bacon

1 lb ground beef

½ cup panko bread crumbs

½ small white onion,
finely chopped

1 egg

3 cloves garlic, minced

2 teaspoons minced
fresh thyme

2 teaspoons minced
fresh rosemary

2 teaspoons dried oregano

½ teaspoon kosher salt

½ teaspoon freshly ground
black pepper

16 oz low-moisture
mozzarella cheese

1 jar (24 oz) of your favorite
marinara sauce

4–6 Kaiser rolls or small
French rolls

Chopped fresh flat-leaf parsley,
for garnish

In the six (almost seven) years of dating my boyfriend, Jared, I've rarely heard him throw around the phrase "one of the best things you've ever made." But these meatball sandwiches are the way to his heart. My Philly-native beau grew up on subs from Wawa and Philly cheesesteaks from some of the best-known places, so I know when it comes to hoagies, he knows his shit. This sub is filled with stuffed cheesy meatballs swimming in marinara sauce, piled high with mozzarella, and baked to perfection. Serve alongside a warm bowl of extra marinara for dipping, and an ice-cold beer.

SERVES 4–6

In a large sauté pan over medium heat, cook bacon for about 5–6 minutes, until fat has rendered off and bacon is crisp. Transfer to a paper towel–lined plate to drain, then chop finely.

In a large mixing bowl, combine ground beef, panko, onion, egg, garlic, thyme, rosemary, oregano, salt, and pepper. Mix well until all ingredients are combined.

Preheat oven to 350°F.

Cut half of the mozzarella log into fifteen ½-inch pieces. Grate the remaining mozzarella cheese and set aside. Use meat mixture to form 1- to 2-inch meatballs around the mozzarella pieces. Continue to mold all the meatballs. Drain most of the bacon grease from the pan, until just enough remains to lightly coat the pan. Place pan over medium heat and cook meatballs, turning once, for 8–10 minutes, or until meatballs are crispy and cooked through. Add in a jar of marinara sauce, stir to combine, and bring to a low simmer. Remove from heat.

Slice open rolls and place onto a baking sheet. Add 3–4 meatballs to each roll, along with a few tablespoons of sauce. Top each with a handful of shredded mozzarella cheese. Melt in the oven for 8–10 minutes, or until the cheese is gooey and melty on top. Garnish with chopped parsley and serve right away.

Cashew Nut Chicken

½ cup soy sauce

1 tablespoon honey

2 tablespoons Thai sweet red chile sauce

2 teaspoons sambal oelek chile paste

1 teaspoon minced garlic

1 teaspoon minced ginger

1 teaspoon sesame oil

1½ tablespoons olive oil

2 lb boneless, skinless chicken breast, cut into 1-inch cubes

Kosher salt

1 red or green bell pepper, chopped

3 green onions, cut into 2-inch lengths + more, thinly sliced (for topping)

⅓ cup chicken stock

2 tablespoons cornstarch

1 can (8 oz) water chestnuts, drained

¾ cup whole unsalted roasted cashews

Steamed rice, for serving

Bring your favorite Thai restaurant home with this flavor-filled cashew nut chicken. This dish is as simple as any stir-fry but elevated with classic, sprightly Thai flavors. Serve alongside a bowl of rice and accompanied with your favorite bottle of wine for an easy date night with your darling.

SERVES 4

In a small bowl, whisk together soy sauce, honey, chile sauce, chile paste, garlic, ginger, and sesame oil until combined.

In a large, heavy-bottomed frying pan over medium-high heat, heat olive oil for 1–2 minutes. Add in cubed chicken in an even layer and sprinkle with salt. Cook for 3–5 minutes on each side, until cooked through.

Add in bell pepper and green onions and cook for 2–3 minutes. Drizzle in the chicken stock to deglaze the pan, scraping the brown bits from the pan bottom.

Lower your heat to medium-low and add in two-thirds of the sauce mixture and stir. Add in 2 tablespoons of cornstarch to the remaining one-third of the sauce and whisk together. Pour mixture over the chicken and let simmer for 2–3 minutes, or until sauce has thickened. If the sauce is too thick, dilute with water as needed.

Add in water chestnuts and whole roasted cashews and stir together to coat everything with sauce.

Serve topped with more green onions, with steamed rice alongside.

Miso Carbonara

8 oz bacon, chopped into 1-inch pieces

1 bunch lacinato (Tuscan) kale, stems removed and leaves chopped

2 tablespoons white miso paste

2–3 teaspoons sriracha sauce, or to taste

2 large eggs

1 egg yolk

1 teaspoon freshly ground black pepper

1 cup grated Parmesan cheese + more for serving

½ lb dried or fresh spaghetti noodles

I firmly believe that pasta is one of the love languages of the world. I'm going out on a very long limb here and saying this may be my favorite recipe in the book. (But don't quote me after I've had a few miso chocolate chip cookies (page 237). I've got a thing for miso, okay?!) This. Carbonara. Is. Everything. It's melt-in-your-mouth, ultra-umami creaminess in every tender bite. This is what you NEED to make if you're trying to impress someone. It requires less time to make than it will take you to get yourself primped for the date. I can't wait to hear how your night goes after this one.

SERVES 2–3

In a frying pan over medium heat, cook bacon until fat has rendered off and bacon is crisp. Remove with a slotted spoon and place onto a paper towel–lined plate. In the same frying pan, add in chopped kale and cook, stirring frequently, until wilted, about 2–3 minutes. Remove pan from heat and set aside.

In a medium bowl, whisk together miso paste, sriracha, eggs, egg yolk, pepper, and Parmesan cheese until smooth.

Bring a large pot three-fourths full of salted water to a boil over high heat. Add the pasta, stir well, and cook according to package directions for al dente. Drain, reserving 1 cup pasta water.

Add the hot, cooked al dente pasta and three-fourths of the bacon (save some for topping) to the frying pan with kale. Add in miso-egg mixture and the ½ cup pasta water to the pasta. Toss everything well to coat until the mixture is silky and cheesy. The residual heat from the noodles will cook the eggs.

Divide among bowls and top with extra Parmesan cheese and pepper.

Lobster Mac & Cheese

2–3 lobster tails (3 if you want it very meaty)

½ lb macaroni pasta

3 tablespoons unsalted butter (divided) + more for pan

2 cloves garlic, minced

2 tablespoons all-purpose flour

1½ cups milk, warmed

Pinch of nutmeg

Pinch of cayenne pepper

½ teaspoon sea salt

½ teaspoon freshly ground black pepper

1½ cups shredded Cheddar cheese

½ cup shredded fontina cheese

½ cup panko bread crumbs

My very first job after college was as an event planner at an extremely swanky private social club in downtown Los Angeles. The hours were long, the commute was longer, and it often left me getting home well past dinnertime. If I could, I'd always sneak a lobster mac and cheese home to Jared (his favorite!) for a late-night treat. Inspired by the classic, this bubbly, cheesy mac and cheese is loaded to the brim with tender lobster meat, and truly presents as something exceptionally posh for date night.

SERVES 4

Bring a medium pot of water (enough to cover the lobster tails) to a boil. Add in lobster tails and cook for 6–8 minutes, or until shells are bright red and meat is opaque. Drain water and place lobster tails in ice water to cool. Remove lobster meat from shells and dice.

Preheat oven to 325°F. Butter a 9 x 13-inch baking dish.

Bring a large pot of salted water to a boil and cook pasta according to package directions for al dente. Drain and set aside.

In a medium saucepan over medium heat, melt 2 tablespoons butter. Add in garlic and cook for 1–2 minutes, or until fragrant. Sprinkle in flour and cook for an additional 1–2 minutes, or until golden.

Slowly whisk warmed milk into flour mixture, stirring constantly for 3–4 minutes, or until sauce is thick enough to coat the back of a spoon. Whisk in nutmeg, cayenne, salt, and pepper.

Whisk in cheeses and stir until melted. Remove from heat and let mixture cool for 10–15 minutes.

Stir cheese mixture, cooked noodles, and lobster together and pour into the greased baking dish.

Melt remaining tablespoon of butter and stir together with panko. Top macaroni and cheese with panko mixture and bake for 25–30 minutes, or until top is golden brown.

Cacio e Pepe Risotto with Shrimp

6 cups chicken stock

5 tablespoons butter

1 large shallot, minced

2 cloves garlic, minced

2 cups arborio rice

¾ cup pinot grigio wine or other dry white wine

2 cups finely grated pecorino or Parmesan cheese + more for topping

Kosher salt and freshly ground black pepper

FOR THE GARLIC-BUTTER SHRIMP TOPPER (OPTIONAL)

4 tablespoons unsalted butter

1 lb shrimp, peeled and deveined

3 cloves garlic, minced

Chopped flat-leaf parsley, for garnish

This risotto was inspired by a meal Jared and I had on a cold, blustery day during our vacation to Italy. We took a boat over to the colorful Island of Burano and ended up hiding out in the trattoria Al Gatto Nero (Black Cat) until the rain cleared. It's a quaint mom-and-pop type of place with a Michelin star reputation. We ordered an array of fresh seafood dishes, chatted about how lucky we felt about this once-in-a-lifetime trip, and practically melted into our bowls of piping hot, extremely creamy risotto. A dish reminiscent of one of my most romantic days, I hope it passes on all the same fuzzy feelings to you.

SERVES 4

In a large saucepan, bring chicken stock to a low simmer. Turn heat down to low and keep broth warm.

In a large sauté pan, over medium heat, melt butter and add in shallot and garlic. Cook for 2–3 minutes, stirring, until shallot has softened.

Add the rice, stir to coat with butter, and cook for 2–3 minutes. Add in white wine, stir, and cook for 1–2 minutes. Add in chicken stock ½ cup at a time, stirring often, and waiting until each addition is absorbed before adding more. Continue until rice is tender and creamy, about 20–22 minutes.

Remove from heat and stir in cheese, 2 teaspoons pepper, and salt to taste. Serve in shallow serving bowls and top with additional grated Parmesan cheese.

To make the optional shrimp topper, in a medium sauté pan over medium-high heat, melt butter. Add in shrimp and season evenly with salt and pepper. Sauté for 3–5 minutes, or until shrimp are opaque and pink in color. Add in garlic and cook for 1 additional minute, or until fragrant. Spoon shrimp onto risotto and sprinkle with fresh parsley before serving.

Sexy Siam Salad

FOR THE DRESSING

2 tablespoons rice wine vinegar

¼ cup olive oil

2 tablespoons Thai sweet red chile sauce

2 tablespoons soy sauce

1 tablespoon fresh lime juice

1 tablespoon honey

1 teaspoon sesame oil

1–2 teaspoons sriracha sauce

2 teaspoons fresh ginger, peeled and minced

FOR THE SALAD

3 cups thinly sliced napa cabbage (½ head)

3 cups thinly sliced red cabbage

½ cucumber, thinly sliced

¼ cup fresh mint leaves, torn

½ cup fresh cilantro, chopped

½ cup fresh basil leaves, torn

3 green onions, sliced diagonally

1 cup mandarin oranges, canned in water with no added sugar

¼ cup roasted peanuts

½ cup store-bought crisp fried onions

1 avocado, thinly sliced

I know what you're thinking. A salad in the date night chapter? The answer is, absolutely. Honestly, I'd eat this Thai-inspired salad any day of the week but I find it exceptionally special. One bite and you'll realize that the mingling of sweet and savory flavors will have your taste buds dancing. Pair with my Oven-Baked Hot Honey Chicken Tenders (page 138) for one of the best chicken salads you'll ever have.

SERVES 4–6

To make the dressing, in a small jar, shake together rice wine vinegar, olive oil, chile sauce, soy sauce, lime juice, honey, sesame oil, sriracha, and ginger. Refrigerate until serving.

To make the salad, in a large serving bowl, toss together napa cabbage, red cabbage, cucumber, mint leaves, cilantro, basil leaves, and green onions. Add in half the dressing and toss together. Top the salad evenly with mandarin oranges, roasted peanuts, fried onions, and avocado slices. Serve with the remaining dressing on the side.

Saucy Red Wine Short Ribs

2 tablespoons vegetable oil

3–4 lb beef short ribs

Kosher salt and freshly ground black pepper

2 small yellow onions, chopped

2 shallots, chopped

3 medium carrots, peeled and chopped

2 celery ribs, chopped

3 tablespoons all-purpose flour

3 tablespoons tomato paste

2 cups dry red wine, like cabernet sauvignon

2 cups beef stock (chicken stock will also work)

5 thyme sprigs

2 rosemary sprigs

1 garlic head, cut in half lengthwise

Chopped fresh flat-leaf parsley, for garnish

These melt-in-your-mouth short ribs are simmered in a rich red wine sauce until they are fall-off-the-bone tender. While they may seem extra luxurious, they're super easy to prep, and cook low and slow in the oven. Perfect for those extra-chilly nights where leaving your living room hibernation is non-negotiable. Serve them up coffee table–style with plenty of cozy blankets and red wine for an easy, yet memorable winter evening.

SERVES 4–5

Preheat oven to 350°F.

In a large Dutch oven over medium-high heat, heat vegetable oil. Pat short ribs dry with paper towels and sprinkle evenly with salt and pepper.

Working in 2 batches, sear short ribs on each side for about 3–4 minutes, or until crusted and golden brown. Transfer short ribs to a plate and set aside.

Add in onions, shallots, carrots, and celery to Dutch oven, season evenly with salt and pepper, and cook for 5 minutes. Sprinkle in flour and tomato paste, stir together, and cook for 2–3 minutes.

Stir in red wine and cook for 2–3 minutes. Transfer short ribs back to the pot. Bring to a simmer and simmer for 10–15 minutes.

Add beef stock, herbs, and garlic head to the mixture. Cover the pot and transfer to the oven. Braise for 2–2½ hours, or until the short ribs begin to fall off the bone.

Skim fat off the top and discard. Taste test sauce for salt and pepper and season accordingly. Serve ribs with sauce spooned over, garnished with parsley.

Oven-Baked Hot Honey Chicken Tenders

1 cup honey

1 Fresno chile, thinly sliced

1 teaspoon smoked paprika

1½ lb boneless, skinless chicken breast halves

2 eggs

1½ cups panko bread crumbs

1½ teaspoons kosher salt

½ teaspoon freshly ground black pepper

1 teaspoon garlic powder

Pinch of cayenne pepper

2 tablespoons olive oil

This Nashville-inspired fried comfort food just got a healthier, oven-baked makeover. One of my favorite things to do is take a really decadent recipe and give it a healthier spin for everyday meals. This chicken is great to make when you're looking for something classic and easy. It's crunchy on the outside, succulent on the inside, and drizzled off with a hot honey glaze. Perfect served on its own, but my favorite is on top of my Sexy Siam Salad (page 134). I hope you and your lover find it just as tasty as I do.

SERVES 4

In a small saucepan over low heat, whisk together honey and Fresno chile slices. Heat for 30–40 minutes to infuse the flavors. After the flavors have infused, whisk in the smoked paprika and keep honey warm while preparing chicken.

Cut chicken breasts into long, tender-size pieces.

Preheat oven to 400°F. Line a large baking sheet with parchment paper, place an oven-safe rack on it, spray rack with oil or nonstick spray, and set aside.

In a shallow bowl, whisk together eggs and set aside.

In another shallow bowl, combine panko, salt, pepper, garlic powder, cayenne, and olive oil. Mix together until crumbs are coated evenly with olive oil; this will help the chicken become crisp and golden.

Dip chicken tender pieces one by one into eggs, and then dredge in crumb mixture, pressing the crumbs into each piece. Transfer dredged chicken pieces onto the rack, making sure there are 2 inches in between each chicken piece. Sprinkle any remaining crumb mixture onto the chicken pieces.

Bake chicken for 15 minutes. Flip chicken pieces and continue to bake for an additional 10–15 minutes, or until chicken is crispy and cooked through.

Drizzle warm hot honey over chicken tenders before serving.

Wing Night

FOR THE WINGS

2 lb chicken wings

Olive oil

1 tablespoon brown sugar

1 teaspoon kosher salt

1 teaspoon garlic powder

1 teaspoon onion powder

1 teaspoon paprika

Freshly ground black pepper

FOR THE SAUCE

1 tablespoon unsalted butter

⅓ cup hot sauce (such as Frank's Red Hot)

1 tablespoon honey

¼ teaspoon cayenne pepper

¼ teaspoon garlic powder

FOR SERVING

Celery sticks

Carrot sticks

Ranch or blue cheese dressing

I'm not sure if there is anything sexier to Jared than me standing there with a fresh platter of these wings. Thanks to the rub, there is just enough caramelization that the edges of the wings get crispy and sweet and salty. It's the perfect blend of crisp on the outside and juicy meat on the inside, without ever being fried. I always feel like I've won a great kitchen battle when I manage to make something that is dangerously delicious but WAY healthier than a normal version.

SERVES 2-4 (2 AS A MEAL, 4 AS AN APPETIZER)

Preheat oven to 400°F. Line a baking sheet with foil and place an oven-safe cooling rack on top. Cooking the chicken on top of a cooling rack will help the wings ventilate and crisp up without frying, so don't skip this step!

To make the wings, pat chicken wings dry with paper towels and place in a large bowl. Drizzle evenly with olive oil.

In a small bowl, whisk together brown sugar, salt, garlic powder, onion powder, paprika, and a few turns of the pepper mill. Rub the dry mixture all over the chicken wings. Transfer chicken wings to rack on prepared baking sheet. Bake for 45–50 minutes, flipping the chicken wings halfway through cooking time. Let wings rest for 5 minutes before coating in sauce.

To make the sauce, in a small saucepan over medium heat, combine butter, hot sauce, honey, cayenne, and garlic powder. Cook for 5 minutes, whisking frequently, until sauce has thickened and reduced slightly.

In a large bowl, toss wings with sauce mixture until all wings are well coated. Serve with celery sticks, carrot sticks, and ranch or blue cheese dressing.

Cook's Tip: If you're short on time, feel free to use your favorite premade buffalo sauce. Use ¾ cup or enough to coat all the wings. If buffalo sauce isn't your favorite, these are perfect with BBQ sauce or even delicious on their own with just the dry rub.

Do You Want Me to Bring a Side?

Sides are arguably my favorite part of any meal. A memorable side dish should be easy to prepare, rich in flavor, and serve in a supporting role of a great meal. Each one of these recipes is a loyal sidekick that will be there for you for any occasion. Turn up with one of these dishes and you'll be everyone's favorite guest.

Rosemary Focaccia Bread

3 tablespoons olive oil for dough + more for pan and drizzling

1½ cups warm water (110°–115°F)

1 tablespoon honey

1½ teaspoons kosher salt

3½ cups all-purpose flour

1 packet (2¼ teaspoons) active dry yeast

Rosemary needles

Flaky sea salt, for topping

Truthfully, I think baking homemade bread takes a level of patience I probably won't ever achieve in life. If there is one loophole to this (or you're a bread master...if so, let's be pals) it's focaccia. Believe me when I tell you that you quite literally throw all the ingredients into a mixer, dump the dough onto a baking sheet, and slather it with delicious olive oil, rosemary, and flaky sea salt. So easy. I'm drooling just thinking about that first fresh, hot, heavenly bite.

SERVES 6–8

Grease a 9 x 13–inch rimmed baking sheet generously with olive oil and set aside.

In the bowl of a stand mixer fitted with the dough hook (or in a large mixing bowl with a handheld mixer) combine warm water, olive oil, honey, salt, flour, and yeast. Mix together for 60 seconds; the dough will be very sticky.

Pour the dough onto your prepared baking sheet, cover with a cloth, and let rise for 1 hour in a warm, dry place (I usually place mine in the unheated oven).

When the dough is almost finished rising, preheat oven to 375°F.

Poke holes in the top of the dough with your fingers and drizzle lightly with olive oil. Scatter with fresh rosemary needles and flaky sea salt. Bake for 25–30 minutes, or until top is golden brown. Serve warm or at room temperature.

Garlicky Charred Super Greens

1 bunch of lacinato (Tuscan) kale, ribs trimmed

8 oz green beans, trimmed

8 oz broccolini, leaves and stems trimmed

1 bunch green onions

2–3 teaspoons canola or avocado oil

½ teaspoon crushed red pepper flakes

2 cloves garlic, minced

Flaky sea salt and freshly ground black pepper

This green power-packed healthy dish is inspired by one from an amazing Indian restaurant, Dishoom, in London. My best friends and I waited two hours for a table at this restaurant and I walked away having eaten one of the best side dishes I've ever had. These greens are simply charred and tossed in aromatic raw garlic, and complement just about any protein you care to pair with them.

SERVES 2-4

Pat veggies dry and place in a large mixing bowl. Drizzle with oil and toss well.

Heat a cast-iron frying pan or wok over medium-high heat. Add the greens in 2 or 3 batches and cook for 6–8 minutes per batch, or until greens are charred.

Toss the greens with red pepper flakes and garlic, and season with ½ teaspoon salt and a few turns of the pepper mill, and serve.

Crispy Smashed Red Potatoes

20 small red potatoes

¼ cup olive oil

2 teaspoons minced garlic

1 tablespoon minced rosemary
+ more for topping

Kosher salt and freshly ground
black pepper

Chopped fresh flat-leaf parsley

This one goes out to all you picky eaters and carb lovers—you know who you are. And we all have that friend or relative who just isn't into a little bit of spice or anything outside of a certain color palette. For me, that's my sweet brother. It's always been a bit of a challenge to create something that satisfies both of our palates, but this recipe has proven to be pure gold for our relationship. Crispy smashed red potatoes—tender on the inside and salty, golden-brown on the outside. I'm convinced there's not a soul on this planet that this combination doesn't resonate with.

SERVES 4-6

Preheat oven to 450°F.

Scrub potatoes clean and place in a large stockpot. Fill pot halfway with water. Bring to a boil, reduce to a rolling simmer, and cook for an additional 10–12 minutes, or until the potatoes are fork-tender.

Drain the potatoes and transfer to a large sheet pan.

In a small bowl or cocktail mixing glass, whisk together olive oil, minced garlic, and minced rosemary.

With a heavy drinking glass or measuring cup, gently smash the potatoes down until they have split open. Brush olive oil mixture evenly over potatoes. Sprinkle evenly with salt and pepper.

Bake for 10–15 minutes, or until potatoes are crispy and golden brown. Sprinkle extra minced rosemary and chopped parsley on top before serving.

Cook's Tip: The potatoes can be boiled and then refrigerated for up to 2 days before roasting.

Caprese Salad 3 Ways: Classic, Fruity & Savory

FOR THE BALSAMIC DRIZZLE

2 cups balsamic vinegar

2 tablespoons pure maple syrup (optional)

CLASSIC

3 ripe tomatoes

12 oz fresh mozzarella

Large bunch of fresh basil leaves

Olive oil

Balsamic drizzle (optional)

Flaky sea salt and freshly ground black pepper

This is hands-down my most-made side dish of summer. Caprese salad is all about using the best-quality ingredients. Whether it's from your garden or the farmers market, go with produce that's local and fresh. Each version of this dish brings something unique so you can incorporate a classic balsamic drizzle, sweet peaches, or savory prosciutto. All the beautiful ingredients come together perfectly to create a simple, elevated summertime salad.

SERVES 3–4

To make the balsamic drizzle, in a small saucepan, combine balsamic vinegar and maple syrup, if using, and bring to a low simmer. Stirring occasionally, gently simmer balsamic vinegar for 10–15 minutes, or until it's reached a pourable syrup consistency. Transfer to a jar or serving bottle and let cool to room temp before using. Balsamic drizzle will stay fresh in the fridge for up to 1 month.

FRUITY

2 yellow peaches, pitted and sliced

2 cups heirloom baby cherry tomatoes, halved

½ red onion, thinly sliced

1½ cups ciliegine (cherry size) fresh mozzarella balls

Olive oil

Balsamic drizzle (optional)

Flaky salt and freshly ground black pepper

Large bunch of fresh basil leaves

SAVORY

3 oz prosciutto, torn

2 ripe tomatoes

12 oz fresh mozzarella

1 avocado, thinly sliced

Large bunch of fresh basil leaves, thinly sliced

Freshly ground black pepper

Balsamic drizzle (optional)

CLASSIC: Slice tomatoes and mozzarella cheese into thick slices (aim for 10–12 slices each). Overlap a repeating pattern of tomato slices, mozzarella slices, and 1–2 basil leaves on a large serving platter. Drizzle with a thin stream of olive oil and balsamic drizzle, if using. Scatter basil leaves on top and sprinkle with flaky salt and pepper.

FRUITY: In a large serving bowl or platter, gently toss together peach slices, halved cherry tomatoes, red onion, and mozzarella balls. Drizzle evenly with olive oil and balsamic drizzle, if using. Sprinkle with flaky salt and pepper and scatter basil leaves on top before serving.

SAVORY: Place a small nonstick pan over medium heat. Add the prosciutto. Let the prosciutto get nice and crispy, about 2–3 minutes per side. Remove prosciutto and drain on paper towels.

Cut tomatoes and mozzarella cheese into thick slices (aim for about 8 slices each). Overlap tomato, mozzarella, and avocado slices on a large serving platter, and crumble crispy prosciutto and scatter sliced basil on top. Finish with pepper and balsamic drizzle, if using.

Crispy Roasted Broccolini

2–3 bunches broccolini florets

3 tablespoons olive oil

3 cloves garlic, minced

1 teaspoon crushed red pepper flakes

Kosher salt and freshly ground black pepper

Fresh lemon juice (optional)

Parmesan cheese (optional)

In all of its "fancy broccoli" glory, this broccolini dish makes even the simplest ingredients shine. Whether you're bringing a side to a dinner party or throwing together a midweek dinner, this light, healthy dish will be a new staple. Easy-to-prep, pairs with practically any meal, and is customizable to your liking—spices, herbs, lemon, or Parmesan!

SERVES 4

Preheat oven to 450°F.

On a rimmed baking sheet, toss broccolini, olive oil, minced garlic, and red pepper flakes together. Make sure that there is enough space between broccolini stalks (use two baking sheets if needed) so that the broccolini stalks will be roasted, instead of steamed.

Sprinkle broccolini with an even layer of salt and black pepper. Roast broccolini for 10–15 minutes, or until tender and slightly crispy.

If you like, drizzle lightly with fresh lemon juice or Parmesan cheese right before serving for an extra burst of flavor.

Radicchio Citrus Salad

FOR THE SALAD

2 navel oranges

1 grapefruit

1 small head radicchio, leaves torn

1 Belgian endive

½ cup fresh cilantro leaves

½ cup pistachios, shelled

½ cup crumbled goat cheese

FOR THE DRESSING

3 tablespoons fresh orange juice

1 tablespoon fresh lemon juice

2 teaspoons honey

2 teaspoons Dijon mustard

¼ cup olive oil

Kosher salt and freshly ground black pepper

Let's get a bit fancy, shall we? I've always felt like this one is simple enough to not cause stress, yet unique enough to feel special. It's like a salad that's almost too pretty to eat, but insanely satisfying. The slices of sweet citrus with flavorful, bitter greens topped with the richness of pistachios and goat cheese—can you think of a more elegant way to start dinner?! She's a showstopper with that "cool girl" kind of ease.

SERVES 4

To make the salad, first peel and slice oranges and grapefruit: for each fruit, cut a thick slice off the top and bottom so some of the fruit's flesh is exposed. On a flat surface, with a sharp paring knife, follow the curve of the fruit to cut away the peel and the white pith, exposing the fruit's flesh. Slice the peeled citrus crosswise into rounds.

On a shallow serving platter, arrange radicchio and Belgian endive leaves. Top with cilantro and gently layer in citrus segments. Top with pistachios and goat cheese.

To make the dressing, in a small bowl or mason jar, whisk or shake together citrus juices, honey, Dijon mustard, olive oil, ¼ teaspoon salt, and pepper to taste until smooth and emulsified.

Drizzle dressing over the salad or serve on the side with a spoon for drizzling.

Lemon, Herb & Feta Orzo Salad

½ lb (8 oz) orzo pasta

1 cup cherry tomatoes, halved

½ red onion, finely diced

1 small cucumber, diced

Juice of 1 lemon

½ cup olive oil

Kosher salt and freshly ground black pepper

½ cup chopped basil + basil leaves for garnish

4 oz feta cheese, crumbled

Lemon slices, for garnish

The standout dish that always gets noticed, and it's too good not to share. Let's be honest—I'm not the gal who's going to give a boring salad a second glance, so I can promise this one does not disappoint. The feta alone makes the salad, but when you add in veggies, lemon, herbs, and orzo, it's next-level. Not to boast about being the party favorite or anything, but this one does bestow a certain level of popularity!

SERVES 4-6

Bring a large pot of salted water to a rolling boil. Add the orzo and cook for 7-8 minutes, stirring frequently to prevent sticking. Drain pasta, but do not rinse.

In a large serving bowl, toss together orzo pasta, halved cherry tomatoes, red onion, cucumber, lemon juice, olive oil, 2 teaspoons salt, and 1 teaspoon pepper until combined.

Gently stir in chopped basil and feta cheese. Taste test for salt and pepper and season accordingly. Salad can be served at room temp, or can be made the night before and refrigerated (let sit at room temperature for 20-30 minutes before serving). Garnish with fresh lemon slices and basil leaves before serving.

Cook's Tip: For leftovers, squeeze a bit more fresh lemon juice and drizzle with olive oil and toss together again before serving.

Roasted Honey Carrots with Chile Oil

FOR THE CARROTS

2 bunches (about 2 lb total) young carrots, trimmed and peeled

2 tablespoons honey

2 tablespoons olive oil

2 teaspoons minced rosemary needles

4 cloves garlic, minced

Kosher salt and freshly ground black pepper

FOR THE CHILE OIL

⅓ cup vegetable oil

1 tablespoon crushed red pepper flakes

Pinch of salt

Opposites attract, and that's always true for that delicious balance of sweet and spicy. This is a perfect wintry dish that brings a bit of brightness and flavor to the table. Drizzle the chile oil on top and keep an extra jar of it to use all season as a casual condiment or an added ingredient in your most-loved recipe. An easy way to turn up the heat and spice up winter months!

SERVES 4

Preheat oven to 425°F.

Line a large baking sheet with parchment paper and set aside. Cut carrots on the diagonal, or leave whole if they are smaller. Scatter evenly on sheet pan.

In a small bowl, whisk together honey, olive oil, rosemary, and garlic until smooth. Pour over carrots and toss together so carrots are evenly coated. Sprinkle generously with salt and black pepper.

Roast carrots for 35–45 minutes, or until golden brown. About 15–20 minutes into roasting, stir carrots once to ensure even cooking and caramelization.

Meanwhile, make the chile oil. In a small pot over medium-low heat, heat the oil, red pepper flakes, and salt, stirring often, for about 5 minutes. Keep a close watch on oil to prevent smoking or boiling. Slowly simmering will allow for the best flavor infusion.

After about 5 minutes, remove from heat and let cool to room temperature. At this point you can strain the mixture, or leave pepper flakes in oil. Transfer infused chile oil into a jar or bottle and seal.

Once carrots have finished roasting, brush remaining honey garlic bits from the pan onto the plated carrots and drizzle with desired amount of chile oil before serving.

Melon Slab Salad with Honey-Lime Drizzle

FOR THE SALAD

2 cups watermelon cubes

1 cup cantaloupe cubes

1 cup honeydew cubes

1 cucumber, peeled and cubed

1 cup cherry or grape tomatoes, halved

8 oz feta cheese, cubed

8–10 small fresh basil leaves

FOR THE DRESSING

3 tablespoons fresh lime juice

1 tablespoon honey

1½ tablespoons olive oil

½ teaspoon salt

½ teaspoon freshly ground black pepper

This is the most haute version of a fruit salad, with a nice, cool spin on that classic that has been in rotation for years. No time to cube everything for a presentation-worthy platter? Don't stress—just toss it into a bowl and it's just as beautiful. You've taken fruit salad from average to a low-key masterpiece.

SERVES 4–5

To make the salad, combine watermelon cubes, cantaloupe cubes, honeydew cubes, cucumber cubes, halved cherry tomatoes, and feta cubes in a serving bowl or arrange flat like a mosaic (see left) on a platter. Top with fresh basil.

To make the dressing, in a mason jar or small bowl, shake or whisk together lime juice, honey, olive oil, and salt and pepper until dressing is smooth and emulsified. Drizzle dressing over salad before serving.

Cook's Tip: I like to buy a big block of feta and cube it at home, so all the ingredients can be the same size.

Koko's Tangy Black Bean Salad

2 cans (15 oz each) black beans, drained and rinsed

1 cup fresh or canned corn

1 yellow or orange bell pepper, diced

1 cup crumbled feta cheese

1 tablespoon apple cider vinegar

1 tablespoon agave nectar

Kosher salt and freshly ground black pepper

Inspired by the best thing I've ever eaten at our pals Koko and Kelly's. I was instantly hooked the first time Koko made this for us. Poolside snack with chips? My favorite. Side for a cookout? Absolutely. Topping for a tostada? Easy. Tangy from the feta cheese, smooth from the black beans, and you'd never guess that it's only 6 ingredients. Equal parts nourishing and refreshing!

SERVES 4–6 AS A SIDE

In a large bowl, stir together black beans, corn, bell pepper, feta cheese, apple cider vinegar, and agave nectar. Taste test and season with salt and pepper.

Serve chilled or at room temp.

Pink Roasted Radishes with Garlic Aioli

FOR THE AIOLI

½ cup mayonnaise

2 cloves garlic, mashed

1 tablespoon olive oil

1 tablespoon fresh lemon juice

Kosher salt and freshly ground black pepper

FOR THE RADISHES

3 lb radishes, trimmed and halved

1½ tablespoons olive oil

Kosher salt and freshly ground black pepper

Chopped fresh flat-leaf parsley, for garnish

I'm here to sing the praises of an unsung hero. Roasted radishes are not only a low-carb replacement for potatoes but they're affordable, tasty, and satisfying all in one. If you love lighter apps or sides that are roasted, give this one a chance. It'll surprise you how well the almost-sweet taste of the crispy radishes complements the garlic aioli. If you want to try it as an app that's dip-friendly, simply serve the aioli on the side! Cheers to vegetables satisfying that comfort food craving.

SERVES 4

To make the aioli, in a small bowl, whisk together mayonnaise, garlic, olive oil, lemon juice, and salt and pepper to taste. Set aside or refrigerate until serving.

Preheat oven to 425°F.

Arrange radishes on a baking sheet and drizzle evenly with olive oil. Sprinkle generously with salt and pepper and toss together.

Roast radishes for 20–25 minutes, tossing halfway through. Radishes should be golden brown and fork tender; if not, bake for an additional 5 minutes.

Transfer to a serving platter and sprinkle with fresh parsley. Serve with garlic aioli on the side, or drizzle on top before serving.

Dad's Bacon-Wrapped Peppers

3 jalapeño chiles

3 Hatch or Anaheim chiles, halved

8 oz cream cheese, at room temp

1½ cups shredded sharp Cheddar cheese

1 tablespoon chopped chives

2 cloves garlic, minced

Sea salt and freshly ground black pepper

16 oz bacon

Oh, my life. My dad—I wish I could adequately explain the joy this man gets out of a Saturday evening in front of the grill. He knows the moment he turns around with a plate full of these pepper beauties that he's winning the crowd. Rightly so. That's where I got my heart for entertaining—sharing the best of what you know with the people you love. In this case, it's spicy, cheesy, bacon-y goodness, and I think that's one of the truest forms of love.

MAKES 12

Soak toothpicks in a small bowl of water for 30 minutes.

Halve and seed the jalapeños and Hatch peppers, keeping the stems intact, and set on a large baking sheet. (If you want your cheese mixture spicy, you could reserve some of the jalapeño seeds to add to it.)

In a small bowl, mix together cream cheese, Cheddar cheese, chives, garlic, ¼ teaspoon salt, and a few turns of the pepper mill until combined. Scoop 1½ tablespoons or so of the cream cheese mixture evenly into each pepper.

Wrap ½–1 strip of bacon around each pepper. Use 1 strip for larger Hatch chiles and ½ strip for jalapeños. Secure peppers with soaked toothpicks. Place chiles in the refrigerator for 10–15 minutes before grilling; this will help the cheese mixture stay intact on the grill.

Prepare a charcoal or gas grill for direct grilling over medium heat, or preheat a grill pan on the stove top. Place the chiles on the grill or a grill pan and cook, open chile side down, for 4 minutes, then gently flip over and cook for another 4 minutes, or until bacon is cooked through.

Cook's Tip: Alternatively, you could roast peppers on a sheet pan in the oven at 400°F for 20–25 minutes, or until the bacon is cooked through.

'Tis the Season

If you're down to host the holidays, this chapter is your one-stop shop for classic dishes with a modern twist. Mains, side dishes, and desserts that all earn a spot on your table—or are great to show up at a holiday party with.

Winter Citrus Punch

1–2 medium Valencia oranges

1–2 medium blood oranges

2 bottles (750 ml each) pinot grigio or other dry white wine

½ cup vodka

½ cup triple sec or other orange liqueur

½ cup fresh citrus juice, strained

¼ cup agave nectar or simple syrup

3 fresh rosemary sprigs

3–4 cinnamon sticks

My go-to batched winter cocktail. This white wine sangria bursting with citrus works great for all the winter holidays. I love making large herb-infused ice cubes for punches and cocktails. They make the whole situation feel a bit more festive, and they're insanely easy to make! Simply stud each ice cube with your favorite herb before freezing.

SERVES 8-10

Slice 1–2 Valencia oranges and 1–2 blood oranges and place in a large punch bowl or pitcher.

Add the 2 bottles wine, vodka, triple sec, citrus juice, agave nectar, rosemary sprigs, and cinnamon sticks and gently stir to combine.

Cover tightly and refrigerate for at least 1 hour or up to overnight. Serve over ice if desired.

Baked Brie with Almonds

1 Brie wheel (8–12 oz)

¼ cup honey

Honeycomb pieces

¼ cup Marcona almonds

4–5 figs, quartered

Rosemary sprigs

Crackers

This easy baked Brie is a great appetizer if you're hosting a small holiday party. While it may be simple, there is some serious "wow" value during that first oozing fresh-from-the-oven Brie slice. Serve with your favorite crackers and Winter Citrus Punch (above) for a festive holiday starter.

SERVES 4-5

Preheat oven to 350°F.

Line a baking sheet with parchment paper and place Brie in the center. Bake for 8–10 minutes. To check if it's ready, gently touch the center of the Brie; it should be very soft.

With a spatula, carefully transfer Brie to a serving plate, drizzle with honey, and top with honeycomb pieces, Marcona almonds, figs, and rosemary sprigs. Serve with crackers.

Vanilla Bean Old-Fashioned

1 vanilla bean

1 teaspoon granulated sugar or
1 sugar cube

3–4 dashes of Angostura bitters

2 oz bourbon

Orange zest strip

Luxardo maraschino cherry

On a cold, wintry evening in Aspen, my guy and I were snowed in with two of our best pals, Katie and Ryan. We were supposed to be at the Winter X Games, but ended up bundled up in our family friend's chalet by the fire for a heated game of Monopoly (my favorite!). Ryan made us traditional, yet memorable old-fashioneds, much like himself. We fought over Illinois and Pennsylvania Avenues and ate snacks for dinner. An evening that felt extremely fancy and totally effortless all at the same time.

MAKES 1 COCKTAIL

Split vanilla bean lengthwise and scrape out half the seeds with a small paring knife. Combine seeds, sugar, and 2 teaspoons warm water in a lowball glass. Mix together with a wooden muddler or spoon until sugar is dissolved. Add bitters to the glass.

Fill glass with 1 large square ice cube or 3–4 regular ice cubes. Pour in bourbon. Stir for 15–20 seconds to chill the cocktail.

Twist orange zest strip to express oils into the glass and then drop zest into cocktail. Top with a cherry or scraped vanilla bean and serve.

Cook's Tip: I love serving this smart classic cocktail with simple snacks like Sweet & Smoky Holiday Nuts (page 177) or cheese crackers for the perfect holiday cocktail hour.

Sweet & Smoky Holiday Nuts

2 tablespoons olive oil + more for pan

4 cups unsalted mixed nuts (I use almonds, pecans, cashews, and Marcona almonds)

⅓ cup pure maple syrup

2 teaspoons crushed red pepper flakes

1½ tablespoons minced fresh rosemary

1½ teaspoons smoked paprika

1½ teaspoons flaky sea salt or kosher salt

These holiday nuts are sweet from pure maple syrup, smoky from paprika, earthy from the rosemary, and a bit spicy from red pepper flakes. They are a little bit of everything and equal parts addicting. Perfect for snacking around the holidays or serving up alongside a festive appetizer board. Easy to make, and ready in 30 minutes or less. Use any and all of your favorite nuts for this simple holiday blend.

SERVES 6

Preheat oven to 350°F. Grease a large rimmed baking sheet with olive oil (or nonstick spray).

In a large bowl, toss together mixed nuts, olive oil, maple syrup, red pepper flakes, rosemary, smoked paprika, and salt.

Transfer nuts to the baking sheet and spread in an even layer. Bake for 20–25 minutes, tossing nuts every 5–10 minutes. Once the nuts are golden brown, remove from the baking sheet and transfer onto parchment paper.

Let the nuts cool for 5–10 minutes, then break into large clusters and place in a serving bowl.

Side Note: I love packaging these up in a mason jar and gifting them with a bottle of bourbon as a host gift or a low-key present around the holidays.

15 Ways to Top a Cracker

1. FREE FALLIN'

Pepper jack, ham, apple butter

2. SWEET & SALTY

Blue cheese and honey

3. THE CHEESECAKE

Graham crackers, sweetened whipped cream cheese, strawberry

4. HOLIDAY HAM

Ham, pineapple, Boursin cheese

5. LET'S GET FIGGY

Goat cheese, fig preserve, thyme sprig

6. THANKSGIVING BITE

Turkey, cranberry sauce, Brie cheese

7. PARIS ON THE GO!

Nutella, banana

8. THE BRUNCH BITE

Crème fraîche, smoked salmon, dill, cucumber

9. NEW YORK HOT DOG

Sausage, hot brown mustard, onion

10. ITALIAN STALLION

Ricotta cheese, salami, pesto

11. CRACKER SANDWICH

Pickle, turkey, Swiss cheese, Dijon mustard

12. FANCY PANTS

Gouda or white Cheddar cheese, Marcona almonds, rosemary, truffle oil

13. PB&J

Crunchy peanut butter and strawberry jam

14. THE FANCY LUNCHABLE

Prosciutto and smoked Cheddar cheese

15. EVERYTHING BAGEL

Cream cheese, everything bagel seasoning, chives

Put down the puff pastry. No matter what the occasion, there are endless ways to top a festive cracker. Try out any of these easy combos for an instant appetizer.

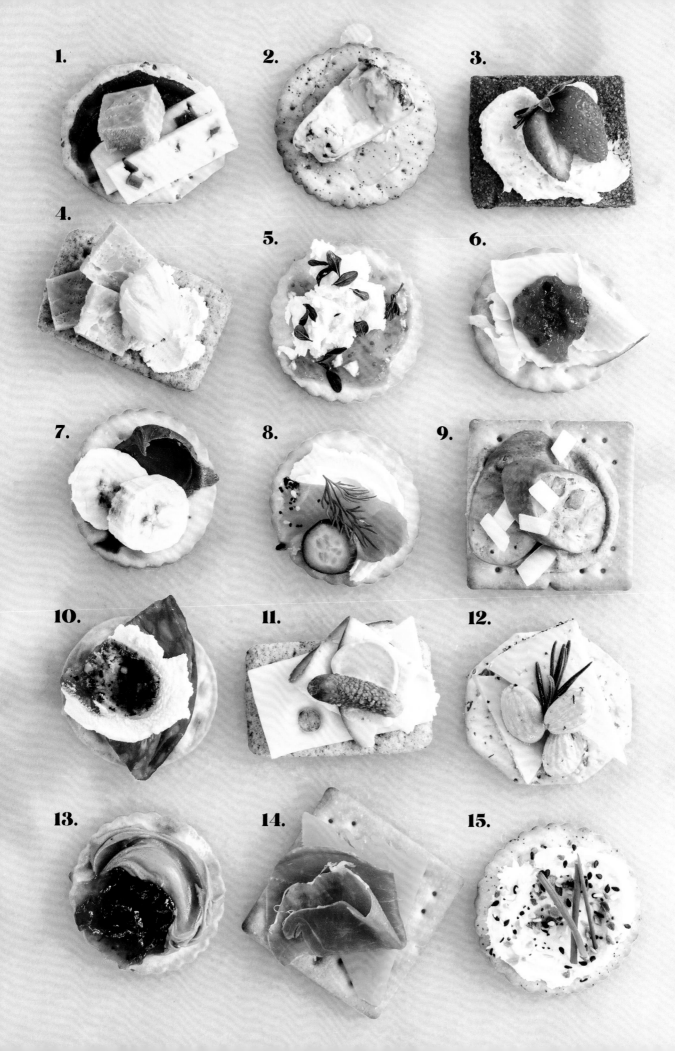

Rosemary-Bourbon Glazed Ham

One 10-lb bone-in, fully cooked, spiral-sliced ham

1 cup brown sugar

¼ cup bourbon or whiskey

2 tablespoons apple cider vinegar

2 tablespoons Dijon mustard

1 orange, zested and juiced

1 tablespoon chopped fresh rosemary needles

½ teaspoon garlic powder

½ teaspoon onion powder

½ teaspoon cinnamon

Freshly ground black pepper

Skip the sugary packaged ham glaze and make something extraordinary from scratch. This glaze takes ten minutes (tops!) to throw together. Filled with rich bourbon notes, fresh citrus zing, and rosemary warmth to complement the sweetness. The trick to a great ham is to not overcook it, because it's already cooked! It just needs warming through. Tent lightly with foil and bake for just about two hours for juicy, glazed spiral-cut holiday ham.

SERVES 8–10

Remove ham from packaging and bring to room temperature for up to 2 hours before baking.

Preheat oven to 325°F. Arrange a rack in the lower third of the oven and remove upper racks.

In a small pot over medium heat, whisk together brown sugar, bourbon, apple cider vinegar, Dijon mustard, orange zest and juice, rosemary, garlic powder, onion powder, cinnamon, and a few turns of the pepper mill. Bring to a low simmer and cook for 5–6 minutes, stirring frequently, until the sugar has dissolved. Remove from heat and set aside.

Place ham in a large roasting pan, face down. Brush half the glaze over the surface of the ham. Loosely cover ham with foil and bake for 1 hour and 30 minutes. During cooking, brush with remaining glaze mixture every 30 minutes. For the last 15 minutes of cooking, remove foil. Let stand up to 30 minutes before transferring to a serving platter.

Get Ahead: You can prep this glaze a couple of days ahead and refrigerate until ready to glaze your ham the day of cooking. Serve with Roasted Maple-Bacon Brussels Sprouts (page 189) and Caramelized Shallot Scalloped Potatoes (page 190) for a rich holiday meal.

Let's Talk Turkey...

How big of a turkey should I buy?

Plan for 1½ pounds of turkey per person: this will give you enough for leftovers! If you're keeping dinner small with 2–4 people, opt for a turkey breast instead.

How long does a turkey need to thaw?

A frozen turkey takes 1 day of refrigerated thaw time per every 4 pounds. A 12-pound turkey will take about 3 days.

Do I have to wash the turkey?

Nope! Don't even worry about it. All you have to do is remove it from the packaging and pat every inch completely dry with paper towels so the skin becomes extra crispy.

What if I don't have a traditional roasting rack?

Crumple up some aluminum foil as a makeshift rack on the bottom of a traditional roasting pan or a disposable roasting pan. This will act as a roasting rack and prop your turkey up so it doesn't sit directly on the bottom of the roasting pan, helping it cook more evenly.

Should I bring the turkey to room temp before cooking?

Take the turkey out of the refrigerator approximately 2 hours before cooking. This will ensure quicker and more even cooking.

What about seasoning?

Honestly, I like to keep it really simple. Creamy butter, fresh herbs, and salt and cracked black pepper go a long way.?

What about trussing?

A real turkey truss is really complicated. I prefer a faux truss where the wings are tucked under the back and the drumsticks are tied together.

Stuffed or unstuffed?

Stuffed is a thing of the past. Not only will you overcook your turkey in order to cook the stuffing, but stuffing in the bird comes out so gummy. Skip it and try my Apple-Pecan Dressing (page 186); you can't go wrong. Opt for aromatics like apples, onions, lemons, and herbs inside the bird for more flavor!

How long?

A turkey will cook for 15 minutes per pound in a 325°F oven. A 12- to 14-pound bird will roughly cook for 3–3½ hours.

What about tenting?

Once the thickest part of the turkey thigh (away from bone) registers 165°F on a meat thermometer, remove from the oven, tent your turkey with foil for 15–45 minutes, then proceed to carve.

Easy Herb-Roasted Turkey

1 whole turkey, 14–16 lb, at room temp

¼ cup unsalted butter, melted

¼ cup minced fresh sage

¼ cup minced fresh rosemary

2 tablespoons fresh thyme, stems removed

Kosher salt and freshly ground black pepper

2 medium apples, quartered

2 yellow onions, quartered

2 celery ribs, chopped

2 cups chicken or turkey stock

Side Note: See Let's Talk Turkey (page 182) for all my best tips, tricks, and how-to's when it comes to cooking a turkey.

Would you believe me if I told you that you could have an amazing roasted turkey with just a few fresh herbs, tons of butter, and a generous amount of salt and pepper? Turkey can often be seen as an intense project with five-gallon Home Depot buckets of brine, arduous deep frying or, even, one of those weird plastic roasting bags. I'm here to tell you, keep it simple, sister. Season and roast until the darkest and thickest part of the turkey reaches 165°F (this is key!) and you'll have a perfectly crisp, juicy bird.

SERVES 10

Arrange a rack in the lower third of the oven and remove upper racks. Place a roasting rack in the center of a large roasting pan (traditional or disposable). Preheat oven to 325°F.

Place your turkey on a large baking sheet or cutting board to prep. Remove turkey neck and giblets from cavity and let bird sit at room temperature. After your turkey has been out of the refrigerator for 2 hours, pat the cavity and the outside of the turkey dry with paper towels. Gently loosen the skin on the breast and legs by gently running your hand between the meat and the skin to separate without tearing. Transfer turkey to prepared roasting pan.

Pour and brush melted butter evenly into the cavity of the turkey and all over the outside skin and underneath the loosened breast and leg skin.

In a small bowl, mix together fresh herbs and sprinkle evenly into the turkey's cavity and the outside skin. Season generously and evenly with salt and pepper.

Tie turkey legs together with kitchen twine and tuck wings underneath the turkey. Place apple quarters, onion quarters, and celery in the cavity and around the turkey. Pour chicken or turkey stock into the bottom of the roasting pan.

Roast, uncovered, for 3–3½ hours, basting the turkey every 30 minutes with pan drippings. To test for doneness, insert a meat thermometer into the thickest part of the thigh, not touching the bone, to see if it registers at least 165°F. Begin to check after 2½ hours.

When the turkey is ready, transfer it to a clean cutting board and let rest for at least 30 minutes before carving.

Apple-Pecan Dressing

1 loaf French bread, cubed

8 tablespoons unsalted butter (divided)

1 medium yellow onion, diced

2 celery ribs, diced

Kosher salt and freshly ground black pepper

1 Honeycrisp apple, diced

1 tablespoon fresh sage, minced

1 tablespoon fresh rosemary, minced

½ tablespoon fresh thyme leaves, stems removed

½ cup dried cranberries

¾ cup pecans

3 cups chicken stock

My favorite Thanksgiving side dish is a tie between green bean casserole and this apple-pecan dressing. While this is hard for me to admit, this dressing might just be the winner on my Thanksgiving sides bracket. It's perfect served alongside turkey, pork tenderloin, or roasted chicken. It's packed with fall flavors like apples, cranberries, pecans, and three different herbs. Swap out the chicken broth for veggie broth for a vegetarian meal.

SERVES 8

Preheat oven to 350°F. Line a baking sheet with parchment paper and spread bread cubes out into one even layer (you may need two baking sheets). Toast for 8–10 minutes, or until lightly golden.

In a sauté pan over medium heat, melt 4 tablespoons butter. Add in onion, celery, 1½ teaspoons salt, and pepper to taste. Cook for 5–6 minutes, or until onion is translucent. Add in apple and cook for another 3–4 minutes, or until tender.

In a large bowl, toss together toasted bread, onion mixture, herbs, cranberries, pecans, chicken stock, and remaining 4 tablespoons melted butter.

Place stuffing in a large casserole dish, cover with foil, and bake for 20 minutes. Uncover and bake for an additional 20–30 minutes, or until golden brown.

Cook's Tip: Use brioche or challah loaf for a richer, buttery flavor.

Roasted Maple-Bacon Brussels Sprouts

FOR THE BRUSSELS SPROUTS

2 lb brussels sprouts

8 oz bacon, diced

3 tablespoons olive oil

Sea salt and freshly ground black pepper

FOR THE MAPLE-BALSAMIC GLAZE

3 tablespoons balsamic vinegar

3 tablespoons pure maple syrup

Sea salt

These simple roasted maple-bacon brussels sprouts are tender on the inside and crusted with salty crispiness on the outside. Right before serving, drizzle them with a sweet maple-balsamic glaze. If you're serving these for a holiday dinner, everything can be prepped ahead of time and baked off before the main meal.

SERVES 4

Preheat oven to 425°F.

Trim and halve brussels sprouts. Pat dry with paper towels so the sprouts will crisp up and brown. Arrange sprouts evenly over one or two baking sheets so they have room in between each other. Distribute bacon evenly over sprouts. Drizzle with olive oil and sprinkle with a pinch of salt (the bacon will also add salt), and pepper to taste.

Roast for 15 minutes. Remove from the oven and toss brussels sprouts to ensure even cooking. Return to the oven for 5–10 minutes, or until sprouts are browned and bacon is crispy.

While brussels sprouts are roasting, prepare maple-balsamic glaze. Heat a small saucepan over medium heat. Add balsamic vinegar, maple syrup, and a small pinch of salt. Simmer, stirring frequently, until mixture thickens into a glaze, about 5 minutes.

Drizzle maple-balsamic glaze over brussels sprouts before serving.

Caramelized Shallot Scalloped Potatoes

3 tablespoons olive oil

6 medium shallots, thinly sliced

Sea salt and fresh black pepper

¼ cup unsalted butter + more for pan

5 cloves garlic, minced

¼ cup all-purpose flour

1 cup milk, warmed

1 cup heavy cream, warmed

1 tablespoon rosemary, minced

1 cup shredded Gruyère cheese (divided)

1½ cups shredded Cheddar cheese (divided)

4 medium russet potatoes

Cook's Tip: It may be tempting to use pre-shredded cheese, but buy a block instead. Fresh cheese melts more evenly and will be way smoother.

As far back as I can remember, we always ate honey-baked ham and some kind of cheesy side dish for Christmas and Easter. My family alternated between macaroni and cheese and what my Mom called "cheesy potatoes," which were my all-time favorite. These caramelized scalloped potatoes are a bit fancier, with caramelized shallots and two kinds of cheeses, but are every bit as creamy and classic.

SERVES 8–10

In a large, heavy-bottomed Dutch oven over medium-low heat, heat olive oil. Add shallots and season with salt and pepper. Cook, stirring occasionally, for about 25–30 minutes, until shallots have become totally softened and caramelized with golden-brown fried edges. Set aside.

Preheat oven to 400°F. Grease a 9 x 13–inch casserole dish with butter (or nonstick spray) and set aside.

In a medium saucepan over medium heat, melt butter. Add garlic and cook for 1–2 minutes, or until fragrant. Whisk in flour and cook, stirring for about 1–2 minutes, until smooth and golden in color.

Slowly add in milk and heavy cream, whisking as you pour. Add 1½ teaspoons salt, ½ teaspoon pepper, and rosemary. Cook for 3–4 minutes, stirring often, until mixture is thick enough to coat the back of a wooden spoon. Remove cream mixture from heat and whisk in ¾ cup shredded Gruyère and 1 cup shredded Cheddar cheese until smooth.

Peel and slice potatoes as thinly as possible, using a mandoline if available. Layer one-third of the potatoes in the greased casserole dish slightly overlapping each other; top with one-third of the caramelized shallots and one-third of the cheese sauce. Repeat to make two more layers.

Cover with foil and bake for 40 minutes, or until potatoes are tender. Remove foil and sprinkle with remaining ¼ cup of Gruyère and ½ cup Cheddar cheese. Return potatoes to the oven and cook for an additional 20–25 minutes, or until the cheese is golden brown and bubbly.

Mashed Sweet Potatoes with Brown Sugar Crunch

FOR THE FILLING

5 medium sweet potatoes

2 tablespoons unsalted butter + more for pan

½ cup packed brown sugar

1 teaspoon ground cinnamon

½ cup whole milk

1 large egg

½ teaspoon kosher salt

½ teaspoon pure vanilla extract

FOR THE TOPPING

2 cups crushed cornflakes

½ cup chopped pecans

1 tablespoon brown sugar

3 tablespoons butter, melted

½ teaspoon cinnamon

1–2 cups mini marshmallows

If you love a nostalgic take on recipes, this class Thanksgiving side dish was made for you. The filling consists of freshly mashed, gently spiced sweet potatoes, topped with a crunchy, brown-sugary cornflake topping for the ultimate blend of textures. One bite will bring you right back to your golden youthful days watching Saturday morning cartoons and eating a big bowl of cornflakes.

SERVES 8

Preheat oven to 400°F.

To make the filling, scrub and pat dry sweet potatoes. Pierce each sweet potato with a fork all over. Place onto a parchment-lined baking sheet and bake for 1 hour, or until very fork-tender. Allow potatoes to cool a bit before handling, and reduce oven temp to 350°F.

Cut each sweet potato in half and scoop out the sweet potato flesh into a medium mixing bowl. Add in butter, brown sugar, cinnamon, milk, egg, salt, and vanilla extract. With a hand masher or electric mixer, mix together potato mixture just until smooth and creamy. Transfer sweet potatoes to a buttered 9 x 13–inch pan or medium casserole dish.

To make the topping, in a small bowl, mix together crushed cornflakes, pecans, brown sugar, butter, and cinnamon. Sprinkle mixture on top of sweet potatoes. Bake for 25 minutes. If the cornflakes start to burn, tent the dish with foil.

Remove from oven and scatter marshmallows on top. Bake for an additional 5–10 minutes, or until marshmallows are browned.

Get Ahead: Prep your sweet potato mixture a day or two before and top off with the cornflake mixture right before baking.

Christmas Morning Eggnog Cinnamon Rolls

FOR THE ROLLS

1 packet (2¼ teaspoons) active dry yeast

1 cup eggnog, warmed (105–110°F)

2 eggs, at room temp, slightly beaten

½ cup butter, melted

4½ cups all-purpose flour + more for dusting

1 teaspoon kosher salt

½ cup granulated sugar

¼ cup butter, at room temp + more for greasing

1 cup packed brown sugar

2½ tablespoons ground cinnamon

1 teaspoon grated nutmeg

FOR THE ICING

½ cup unsalted butter, at room temp

8 oz cream cheese

1 teaspoon pure vanilla extract

4½ cups powdered sugar

¼ cup eggnog

¼ teaspoon kosher salt

1 teaspoon cinnamon

Cook's Tip: If you're not an eggnog lover, simply replace with milk for a just-as-delicious classic cinnamon roll.

It seems as if Christmas morning could be a holiday in its own right. With an agenda including matching pajamas, dog sweaters, festive music, copious amounts of wrapping paper everywhere, and maybe a few Christmosas. Whether I'm in my own little home with boyfriend Jared and dog Rascal or with our immediate family, I am always hopeful for warm, fluffy cinnamon rolls covered in icing. Eggnog cinnamon rolls are soft, fluffy, and infused with eggnog for a subtle, yet festive holiday flair. Prep the rolls the night before and have your home oozing with fresh cinnamon roll aromas in the morning.

SERVES 8

To make the rolls, dissolve yeast into warm eggnog and let sit for 5–10 minutes. While yeast is activating, in the bowl of a stand mixer fitted with a dough hook (or in a large mixing bowl with a handheld mixer) combine eggs, melted butter, flour, salt, and granulated sugar. Add in yeast-eggnog mixture.

Knead with dough hook for about 5–6 minutes, or until dough has come together into a ball. Transfer dough to a greased bowl and cover with a kitchen towel. Place dough in a dry, warm place to rise (I usually place mine in an unheated oven). Allow dough to rise for an hour, or until it has doubled in size.

Preheat oven to 350°F. Butter a 9 x 13-inch casserole dish or a Dutch oven and set aside.

Punch down dough and roll out on a floured surface into a 9 x 15-inch rectangle. Spread evenly with softened butter and sprinkle with brown sugar, cinnamon, and nutmeg. Very gently roll dough up into a log. Cut crosswise slices about 1½ inches thick and arrange snugly in prepared casserole dish. Bake for 25–30 minutes, or until lightly golden on top.

Meanwhile, make the icing. In the bowl of a stand mixer fitted with the paddle attachment (or in a large mixing bowl with a handheld mixer) combine butter, cream cheese, and vanilla extract. Beat for 2–3 minutes. Add in 1 cup of powdered sugar at a time and 1 tablespoon of eggnog after every sugar addition. Add in cinnamon and nutmeg to taste. Spread a thick layer of icing onto warm cinnamon rolls, and serve.

Mom's Apple Pie

FOR THE CRUST

2½ cups all-purpose flour + more for dusting

1 tablespoon granulated sugar

½ teaspoon kosher salt

1 cup (2 sticks) unsalted butter

¼ cup ice water

FOR THE FILLING

½ cup (1 stick) cold unsalted butter

½ cup granulated sugar

½ cup packed brown sugar

2 tablespoons cinnamon

¼ cup all-purpose flour

8 Granny Smith apples

1 egg

2 tablespoons milk

When it comes to food memories, my mom's apple pie is as far back as I can go. I have had this pie every Thanksgiving and Christmas (and sometimes my birthday!) for what seems like the entire twenty-eight years of my existence. Mom, this pie is hands down the most incredible thing you make, and I can't tell you how much I look forward to it year after year. It's stacked extra high with eight large Granny Smith apples, the filling is thick, gooey, and rich in cinnamon, and the crust is so perfectly flaky. It truly embodies what great apple pie should taste like.

SERVES 8

To make the crust, in a large bowl, combine flour, sugar, and salt. With a box grater, shred your two sticks of butter into flour mixture. With a pastry blender or rubbing with your fingertips, blend butter and flour until a crumbly texture forms. Slowly add in your ice water 1–2 tablespoons at a time, incorporating with your hands after each pour. The dough can vary in consistency because of climate (if you live in a dry climate, you may need a little more water, or less in a humid climate). When dough is ready, it will come together in a rough ball; do not overmix.

Form into two disk shapes, wrap in plastic wrap, and refrigerate for at least 2 hours and up to 1 day.

On a well-floured surface, roll out 1 dough disk. The dough may seem tough to roll out, but apply pressure. You want the dough to stay cold, or it will be difficult to move it into the pie dish. Roll your 11-inch dough round around your rolling pin and unroll over your pie dish. Slice butter for filling into 1-tablespoon pats and place 4 single pats evenly on the bottom of the pie shell. Set aside. Preheat oven to 350°F.

To make the filling, in a small bowl, whisk together granulated sugar, brown sugar, cinnamon, and flour and set aside. Peel and core the apples. Cut into thin slices, about ⅛ inch thick, and place in a large bowl of cold water to prevent browning. When finished slicing, drain apples, leaving a small amount of water (about ¼ cup) in the bottom of the bowl. Mix apple slices with three-fourths of the cinnamon sugar mixture, reserving some for the top of the pie. Pour the apples evenly into the prepared pie shell and drizzle juices from the bottom of the bowl on top of the apples. Dollop the remaining 4 pats of butter evenly on top of the apples.

Roll out the other dough round and place on top of apples. Cut a few steam vents across the top with a sharp knife. Seal by crimping the edges as desired. In a small bowl, whisk together egg and milk and brush entire top crust evenly. Sprinkle remaining cinnamon sugar mixture on top.

Bake pie until crust is brown and juices are bubbling. If the edges start to burn, tent gently with foil. Let cool on a wire rack for 1 hour before serving.

Pumpkin Sheet Pan Cake with Toasted Marshmallow Topping

FOR THE CAKE

Nonstick baking spray

2 cups all-purpose flour

2 teaspoons baking soda

1 tablespoon ground cinnamon

¼ teaspoon nutmeg

½ teaspoon salt

1 can (15 oz) pumpkin purée

1½ cups brown sugar

½ cup plain Greek yogurt

½ cup olive oil

2 teaspoons pure vanilla extract

4 large eggs, at room temp

FOR THE TOASTED MARSHMALLOW FROSTING

1 bag (10 oz) mini marshmallows + more for topping (optional)

1 cup (2 sticks) unsalted butter, at room temp

1 teaspoon pure vanilla extract

2¼ cups powdered sugar

2 tablespoons milk

Ground cinnamon (optional)

I'm all about classic pies on Thanksgiving, but for Friendsgiving I love switching things up with a dessert that has a twist. If you love the pumpkin loaf from the coffee shop, you're going to go crazy for this. This pumpkin cake is perfectly spiced, tender, and extremely moist. On top is a thick layer of rich, marshmallow-infused frosting that takes normal buttercream up a huge autumnal notch.

SERVES 10-12

Preheat oven to 350°F. Grease a 9 x 13-inch baking pan or baking dish with nonstick baking spray.

To make the cake, in a mixing bowl, whisk together flour, baking soda, cinnamon, nutmeg, and salt. Set aside. In a separate large bowl, whisk together pumpkin, brown sugar, yogurt, and olive oil until smooth and combined. Whisk in vanilla extract and eggs, one at a time, until just mixed together.

Add the dry ingredients into the wet, mixing until just combined and no large lumps remain. Pour batter into greased baking pan and bake for 35-40 minutes, or until a toothpick inserted in the center comes out clean and the middle of the cake no longer jiggles when the pan is shaken. Let the cake cool for an hour, or until completely cooled. Transfer to a serving dish or leave in the baking pan.

To make the toasted marshmallow frosting, in a nonstick sauté pan over medium heat, heat marshmallows until just melted, about 5 minutes. Set aside to cool.

In the bowl of a stand mixer fitted with a paddle attachment (or in a large mixing bowl with a handheld mixer), combine butter and vanilla extract and beat on high speed for 2-3 minutes, or until mixture is light and fluffy. Stir in cooled marshmallows on medium speed until incorporated. On medium-low speed, add in 1 cup of powdered sugar at a time and 1 tablespoon of milk at a time until incorporated.

Spread frosting on top of the pumpkin cake. Dust with cinnamon and extra marshmallows if desired.

Chocolate-Bourbon Pecan Pie Bars

FOR THE CRUST

¾ cup (1½ sticks) cold unsalted butter, diced + more for pan

1½ cups all-purpose flour

¼ cup sugar

¼ cup finely chopped pecans

5 tablespoons ice-cold water

FOR THE FILLING

⅔ cup brown sugar

6 tablespoons all-purpose flour

1 teaspoon kosher salt

1½ cups corn syrup

4 eggs

1 tablespoon bourbon or whiskey

1½ cups chopped pecans

4 oz bittersweet chocolate, chopped

Every year I make a large, extremely gooey pecan pie for my step-grandfather, Norval. Norval has great taste, especially in his pies. He likes his pecan pie extremely thick and rich with brown sugar filling and not too many pecans. These pecan bars are inspired by him and made extraordinarily decadent with a chocolate and bourbon–infused filling layered on top of a rich shortbread crust. One bite and you won't be able to stop "mmm"ing and longing for a tall cup of coffee.

MAKES 12 BARS

Preheat oven to 350°F. Line a 19 x 13–inch baking pan with parchment paper and grease sides with butter (or nonstick spray).

To make the crust, combine flour, butter, and sugar in the bowl of a stand mixer fitted with the paddle attachment (or in a large mixing bowl with a handheld mixer). Beat at medium speed until the mixture resembles coarse crumbs. Stir in pecans and ice-cold water until mixture starts to stick together.

Press crust mixture evenly onto the bottom of the prepared baking pan. Bake for 18–20 minutes, or until edges are lightly golden brown.

To make the filling, combine brown sugar, flour, and salt in a large bowl, whisking until combined. Add in corn syrup, eggs, and bourbon and mix well. Stir in pecans and chocolate. Spread filling mixture evenly over crust. Bake for 30–35 minutes, or until filling is set when the pan is slightly jiggled.

Let cool completely for 30–40 minutes before slicing into 12 bars.

Tip: If you love gifting cookie boxes for the holidays, these bars are a great addition.

Lazy Brunch

For me, a good brunch is filled with equal parts sweet and savory dishes, is very carefree, and usually ends in a really good afternoon nap #thankyousangriamimosa. All the recipes you will find here are perfect for a simple morning or pair up seamlessly for a more epic spread. I highly recommend starting with the Kale and Sausage Breakfast Pizza and my famous Chocolate Chip Banana Bread.

Bacon-Truffle Deviled Eggs

1 dozen large eggs

1 cup mayonnaise

2 teaspoons Dijon mustard

2 tablespoons truffle oil

Kosher salt and freshly ground black pepper

Pinch of cayenne pepper

Snipped chives, for topping

Crumbled cooked bacon, for topping

Say hello to what I refer to as the Gucci of deviled eggs. Made with lavish ingredients like truffle oil, thick-cut bacon, and, mais oui, Grey Poupon Dijon mustard. These rich and creamy eggs are definitely one of the fanciest recipes in the whole book. Serve with copious amounts of Champagne for an impressive brunch bite.

MAKES 24 PIECES

Place eggs in a large pot and add cool water to cover by 1–2 inches. Bring to a boil, cover pot, remove from heat, and let stand for 8 minutes. Transfer eggs to a bowl of ice water and let stand for 10 minutes before peeling under water. Slice eggs in half lengthwise.

Scoop out egg yolks and place them in a medium mixing bowl. Add in mayonnaise, Dijon mustard, truffle oil, ½ teaspoon salt, a few turns of the pepper mill, and cayenne. With a fork, mash egg yolk mixture together until very smooth and fluffy. Taste test for salt and pepper.

Transfer egg yolk mixture to a piping bag or a lock-top bag with the corner snipped off. Fill each egg white half with 1–2 teaspoons of egg filling mixture.

Garnish each egg with snipped chives and a small piece of bacon.

Sangria Mimosa

2 cups fresh orange juice

½ cup triple sec or other orange liqueur

½ cup vodka

1 orange, halved and thinly sliced

10 mint leaves

1 bottle (750 ml) Champagne, Prosecco, or other sparkling wine, chilled

Warning: This sangria mimosa is so delicious it may induce naps after brunch. Seriously, after a few glasses of this sparkly concoction I can almost guarantee I'll take a nap on the lounge chair outside, but who doesn't love that?! You still get all the great flavor from a regular mimosa, it's just a tad bit stronger and more cocktail-like from the complementing vodka and orange liqueur.

SERVES 6–8

Fill a large pitcher with orange juice, triple sec, vodka, orange slices, and mint leaves. With a muddler, muddle everything together. Refrigerate for 20 minutes.

Top the pitcher off with sparkling wine and gently stir. Serve right away.

Banana-Nut Bread with Chocolate Chips

Nonstick spray for pan

3 very ripe medium bananas + extra slices for topping

½ cup (1 stick) unsalted butter, melted

1 cup brown sugar

2 large eggs

¼ cup milk

1 teaspoon pure vanilla extract

2 cups all-purpose flour

1 teaspoon cinnamon

1 teaspoon baking soda

¼ teaspoon salt

½ cup chopped pecans

1 bag (12 oz) of chocolate chips

I have to brag for a sec, okay?! This banana-nut bread has been made hundreds of times from my blog with five-star reviews and it has earned its way into this cookbook. Anyone I have made this for instantly says it's the best banana bread they've ever had, and for good reason. It's made with extremely ripe mashed bananas for optimum moisture, pecans for a little crunch, and an ENTIRE bag of chocolate chips. Be the morning hero I know you are and make this banana bread for your next morning rendezvous.

SERVES 8–10

Preheat oven to 350°F. Line a 9 x 5–inch loaf tin with parchment paper and spray with nonstick spray.

In a medium bowl, mash ripe bananas until only slightly chunky. Set aside.

In a separate large bowl, combine melted butter and brown sugar, whisking until smooth. Add in eggs, milk, and vanilla extract and whisk until combined. Add mashed bananas to the wet ingredients and fold to combine.

Add flour, cinnamon, baking soda, and salt to the batter and gently stir until combined; do not overmix.

Gently fold in chopped pecans and chocolate chips (reserve ¼ cup for topping) until just combined. Transfer batter to prepared loaf tin and smooth out the top. Top with extra banana slices and chocolate chips.

Bake banana bread for 50–60 minutes, or until a toothpick inserted in the center comes out clean and the top is golden brown.

Let banana bread cool in the pan for 15–20 minutes before transferring to a wire rack to cool completely before slicing.

Caramelized Onion & Goat Cheese Frittata

1 tablespoon unsalted butter + more for greasing

1 small yellow onion, diced

4 oz pancetta, diced

8 eggs

¼ cup milk, half-and-half, or cream

Kosher salt and freshly ground black pepper

½ cup goat cheese

Snipped chives, for topping

Whether you want to call it a quiche or an egg pie, it's damn delicious and SO easy to make. It's got sweet, rich notes from the caramelized onions and salty, creamy bites from the goat cheese. Serve alongside Simple Sophisticated Greens (page 42) for brunch or prep for an easy breakfast to have all week long.

SERVES 6

In a 10-inch oven-safe nonstick or cast-iron frying pan over medium heat, melt butter. Once butter is melted, add in onion and reduce heat to medium-low. Cook, stirring occasionally, for 15–20 minutes, or until onions are golden brown.

Add pancetta to onions and cook for an additional 4–5 minutes, or until crispy.

Preheat oven to 400°F.

In a large bowl, whisk together eggs, milk, ½ teaspoon salt, and a few turns of the pepper mill. Add eggs to frying pan and stir to mix evenly with onions and pancetta.

Dollop egg mixture with goat cheese and cook for 1–2 minutes longer on stove top, or until the edges begin to set.

Transfer frying pan to oven and bake frittata for about 8–10 minutes, or until center is set.

Let frittata cool in the pan for 5 minutes before slicing and serving. Top with snipped chives.

Chai-Spiced Cinnamon Rolls with Espresso Icing

FOR THE ROLLS

1 cup warm water (105–110°F)

1 packet (2¼ teaspoons) active dry yeast

2 eggs, slightly beaten

⅓ cup butter, melted + more for greasing

4½ cups all-purpose flour + more for dusting

1 teaspoon kosher salt

½ cup granulated sugar

FOR THE FILLING

1 cup brown sugar

1½ tablespoons ground cinnamon

1 teaspoon ground cardamom

1 teaspoon ground ginger

½ teaspoon ground cloves

½ teaspoon grated nutmeg

½ teaspoon ground allspice

½ cup (1 stick) butter, at room temp

FOR THE ICING

½ cup (1 stick) unsalted butter, at room temp

1 teaspoon pure vanilla extract

2–2½ cups powdered sugar

4 tablespoons milk

2 teaspoons espresso powder

When I want a real treat in the morning, I skip my cup of coffee and go for a dirty chai latte. These cinnamon rolls embody all of the cozy essence from that creamy, spiced concoction. Fluffy cloudlike cinnamon rolls laced with rich chai-spiced filling and topped with fragrant espresso icing.

MAKES 8 CINNAMON ROLLS

To make the rolls, whisk yeast into warm water. Let sit for 5–10 minutes, or until top is foamy.

While yeast is activating, in the bowl of a stand mixer fitted with a dough hook, combine eggs, melted butter, flour, salt, and sugar. Add in the yeast mixture and knead the dough together on medium-high speed for about 5–6 minutes, or until it has come together into a ball and is soft and supple. Transfer dough to a greased bowl and cover with a kitchen towel. Place dough in a dry, warm place to rise (I usually place mine in an unheated oven). Allow dough to rise for an hour, or until it has doubled in size.

Preheat oven to 350°F. Grease a 9 x 13-inch casserole dish and set aside.

To make the filling, in a medium bowl, mix together brown sugar, cinnamon, cardamom, ginger, cloves, nutmeg, allspice, and softened butter. Set aside.

Punch down the dough and roll out into a 9 x 13-inch rectangle on a floured surface. Spread evenly with filling mixture. Gently roll the dough up into a log and cut 8 crosswise slices about 1½ inches thick. Arrange slices snugly into prepared casserole dish. Bake for 25–30 minutes, or until lightly golden on top. Let rolls cool for 10 minutes before adding icing.

To make the icing, in the bowl of a stand mixer fitted with the paddle attachment (or in a large bowl with a handheld mixer) combine softened butter and vanilla extract. Beat for 2–3 minutes, or until light and fluffy. Add in 2 cups of powdered sugar, 1 cup at a time, plus 2 tablespoons of milk after each addition. Use an extra ½ cup of powdered sugar if a thicker icing is desired. Add in espresso powder and taste test for flavor. Add in more espresso powder if desired. Spread icing evenly over warm cinnamon rolls, and serve.

Cheesy Hash Brown Casserole

½ cup butter, melted + more for dish

1 lb frozen hash browns

8 oz sour cream

1¾ cups chicken stock

2 cups shredded sharp Cheddar cheese

1 small yellow onion, diced

¼ cup milk

Kosher salt and freshly ground black pepper

½ cup chopped green onions

Totally and one hundred percent inspired by the epic hash brown casserole sold at Cracker Barrel. I first had this in college in Colorado and it was almost enough to turn this California girl into a total country chick. I was obsessed. I had never tasted something so cozy, cheesy, and comforting before. This cheesy hash brown casserole makes plenty of appearances on my weekend brunch menu.

MAKES 8-10 SIDE PORTIONS

Preheat oven to 350°F. Lightly grease a 9 x 13-inch casserole dish or 10- to 12-inch cast-iron frying pan and set aside.

In a large bowl, combine hash browns, sour cream, chicken stock, Cheddar cheese, melted butter, yellow onion, milk, ½ teaspoon salt, ½ teaspoon pepper, and half of the green onions.

Pour the contents into the prepared dish and bake for 45–60 minutes, or until top is golden brown. Sprinkle the remaining green onions on top before serving.

Abbie's Earl Grey Scone

½ cup heavy cream + more for brushing tops

2 Earl Grey tea bags

2½ cups all-purpose flour + more for dusting

1 tablespoon baking powder

¾ teaspoon salt

½ cup (1 stick) very cold unsalted butter

3 tablespoons honey

2 large eggs, at room temp

1 teaspoon pure vanilla extract

½ cup chopped dark chocolate

1½ cups powdered sugar

Chopped pistachios, for topping

I travel with my friend and assistant Abbie quite often for work and early-morning photo shoots, and I can always count on her to find us the best coffee and breakfast treat, even in a foreign country. Amongst her favorites are a fresh croissant or a scone. These scones are extremely buttery and filled with notes of Earl Grey tea. On top are a rich tea-infused glaze and pistachios. Pair with an almond-milk latte for a true morning delight.

MAKES 6-8 SCONES

Preheat oven to 400°F and line a baking sheet with parchment paper.

In a small saucepan over medium-high heat, bring heavy cream just to a simmer. Open tea bags, add loose tea to cream, and let steep for 5 minutes off the heat. Strain tea leaves from cream and set cream aside to cool.

In a medium bowl, whisk together flour, baking powder, and salt until well blended. Using a box grater, grate ice-cold butter into flour mixture. With a pastry blender or rubbing with your fingertips, blend flour mixture and butter together until a coarse crumbly texture forms with clumps of butter no larger than small peas.

In another medium bowl, whisk together ¼ cup tea-steeped cream, honey, eggs, and vanilla extract. Gently stir the cream mixture into your flour mixture until just combined. Add chopped chocolate to the batter and gently mix. Be careful not to overmix, or your scones will become tough in texture.

Gently transfer scone dough to a cold, well-floured surface and bring the dough together into a disk about 1 inch thick. Cut the disk into 6-8 triangles. Arrange triangles evenly onto prepared sheet. Brush tops with a light layer of tea-steeped cream and bake for 20-25 minutes, or until the scone tops are golden brown.

To make a glaze, whisk together powdered sugar and 1-2 tablespoons of tea-steeped cream at a time until glaze becomes pourable, using about 2-3 tablespoons cream in all. Pour glaze over scones, sprinkle with pistachios, and serve.

Ultimate Waffle Bar

FOR THE WAFFLES

1 cup all-purpose flour

2 tablespoons sugar

1 teaspoon baking powder

Pinch of kosher salt

1 cup milk

2 large eggs

4 tablespoons (¼ cup) unsalted butter, melted

FOR SERVING

Sliced strawberries

Sliced bananas

Raspberries

Blueberries

Peanut butter

Nutella

Honey

Maple syrup

Whipped cream

Chocolate chips

Powdered sugar

Sprinkles

There is something about a hotel waffle bar that instantly makes me feel like I'm ten years old and on vacation with my parents again. My eyes are already piling up my plate with thick Belgian waffles and a never-ending assortment of toppings. A fun and customizable waffle bar like this is perfect for brunch gatherings like baby showers, engagement parties, and more. The crazier-themed toppings, the better!

SERVES 4–6

Preheat a waffle iron according to manufacturer's instructions.

In a large bowl, whisk together flour, sugar, baking powder, and salt, and set aside. In a separate bowl, whisk together milk and eggs. Gently whisk milk and egg mixture into flour mixture until just combined; do not overmix. Gently whisk melted butter into batter.

For a standard waffle maker, pour about ½ cup of batter into the center of the waffle maker. (For a Belgian waffle iron, follow manufacturer's recommendations.) Close the waffle iron and cook for 2–3 minutes, or until waffles are golden brown and crispy.

On a large platter or serving table, arrange fruits, spreads, and toppings into small bowls and serve with warm waffles.

My Nanna Pam and Papa are the queen and king of brunch, and, luckily, they taught me well. At their house, the bagel bar is the main event. The key is an assortment of fresh bagels and plenty of toppings that let people customize each bagel to their liking. Prep all of your toppings the night before to skip the stressful morning hustle and go straight to enjoying the mimosas.

SERVES 6–8

Arrange bagels, smoked salmon, heirloom tomatoes, cucumbers, red onion, radishes, and lemon on a platter or large wooden cheese board. Place capers and whipped cream cheese into small bowls. Garnish board with fresh dill.

Cook's Tip: Use a mandoline to quickly and evenly slice up your cukes, red onion, radishes, and lemon for the board.

Lox Bagel Bar

6–8 assorted bagels, sliced and toasted

2 lb smoked salmon, thinly sliced

2 heirloom tomatoes, sliced

2 Persian cucumbers, thinly sliced

½ red onion, thinly sliced

3 radishes, thinly sliced

1 lemon, thinly sliced

¼ cup capers, drained (rinsed if salt-cured)

8 oz whipped cream cheese spread

Fresh dill, for garnish

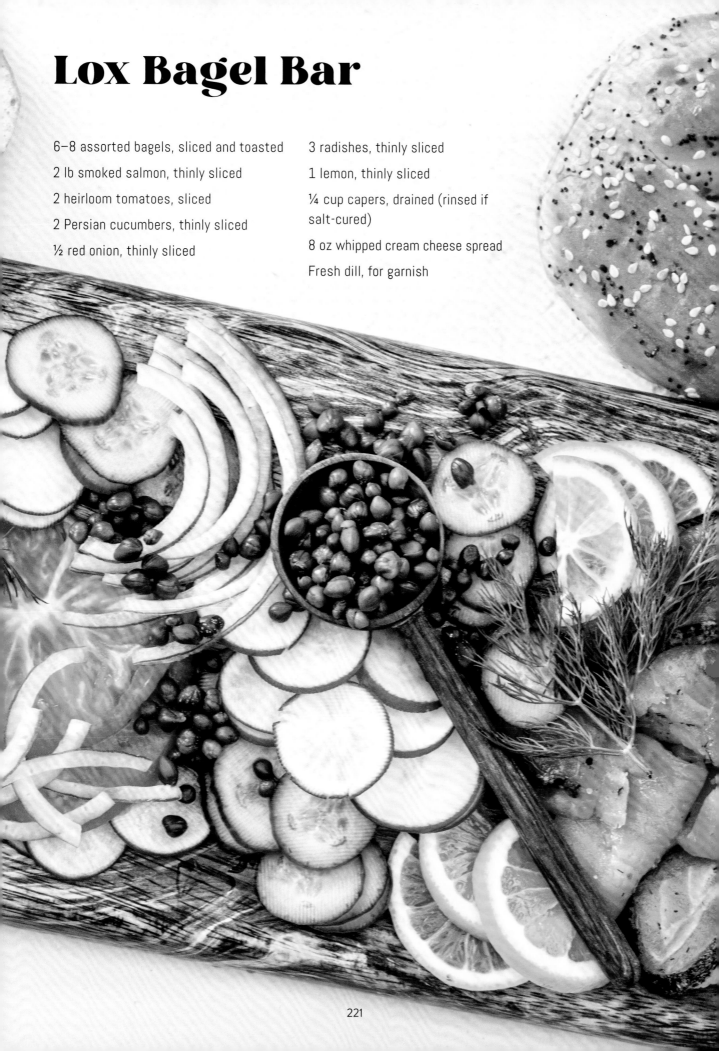

Hangover Breakfast Burritos with Green Salsa

FOR THE GREEN TOMATILLO SALSA

1 lb tomatillos, husked and rinsed

¼ white onion

½–1 jalapeño chile, stem removed, halved

Olive oil

1 clove garlic, roughly chopped

¼ cup chopped fresh cilantro

Juice of 1 lime

1 teaspoon honey

Kosher salt

FOR THE BURRITOS

2½ cups frozen tater tots

½ lb bacon

8 eggs

2 tablespoons milk

Kosher salt and freshly ground black pepper

2 tablespoons olive oil

2 cups Cheddar cheese, grated

6 extra-large flour tortillas

2 small tomatoes, diced

3 avocados, sliced

Green tomatillo salsa, for serving

Sour cream, for serving

Hot sauce, for serving

Designed with your hangover in mind. My best friend, Alex, is the queen at powering through a hangover and told me exactly what I needed inside of these burritos for a true morning cure. Eggs for protein and sustenance, tater tots because fried potatoes are the ultimate hangover food group, and tons of Cheddar cheese and bacon for a little grease. Also, don't forget generous amounts of fresh tomatillo salsa for topping. Serve with ibuprofen and a tall glass of H_2O.

SERVES 6

To make the salsa, preheat oven to 400°F. Place tomatillos, onion, and jalapeño on a rimmed baking sheet. Drizzle with olive oil and rub each ingredient to coat with oil. Roast for 15–20 minutes, or until tomatillos are tender and golden. In a blender or Vitamix, combine roasted tomatillos, onion, jalapeño, garlic, cilantro, lime juice, honey, and salt to taste and blend until smooth. Taste test for more salt once blended. You will have about 2 cups.

To make the burritos, bake tater tots according to package instructions and keep warm. In a frying pan over medium heat, cook bacon until fat has rendered off and bacon is crisp. Remove with a slotted spoon and place onto a paper towel–lined plate. Chop into 1-inch pieces and set aside.

In a bowl, whisk together eggs, milk, 1 teaspoon salt, and a few turns of the pepper mill until light and foamy. In a medium nonstick pan over medium-low heat, heat olive oil and tilt to coat pan. Add in the eggs. Scramble them softly by turning them gently with a silicone spatula. When egg curds start to form, lower heat and cook eggs, turning gently, until they are just cooked through. Remove from heat and top with Cheddar cheese. Place a baking sheet or plate over pan to allow steam to melt cheese.

To assemble the burritos, warm tortillas for a few seconds in the microwave (this helps the folding process) and lay out on a clean surface. Place equal amounts of tater tots, scrambled eggs, and bacon into the center of each tortilla, avoiding the edges. Top with tomato and avocado slices and wrap each burrito up. Heat in a frying pan drizzled with olive oil over medium-low heat for 1 minute on each side. Serve with salsa, sour cream, and hot sauce.

Sheet Pan Chilaquiles

4–6 tablespoons vegetable oil (divided)

12–15 corn tortillas, quartered

Sea salt

1 oz packet ground red New Mexico chile powder

1 teaspoon garlic powder

2 cups chicken stock

5 eggs

TOPPINGS

Cotija cheese, crumbled

1 avocado, sliced

¼ red onion, thinly sliced

¼ cup thinly sliced radishes

½ cup fresh cilantro sprigs

Hot sauce

If you need an easy, pantry staple brunch recipe, chilaquiles is a classic Mexican dish that always hits the spot. I usually have extra tortillas and avocado lying around at all given times and this is the perfect recipe to use them in. This dish is all about the layers, with sauce-soaked freshly fried tortillas, a bed of baked eggs, and fresh toppings like avocado, red onion, radish, cilantro, and hot sauce for a burst of flavor in every bite.

SERVES 4–5

In a large frying pan over medium-high heat, heat 3 tablespoons oil. Add in a fourth or so of the tortilla wedges and cook for 3–5 minutes, flipping once, until they are lightly golden and crispy. Transfer cooked tortillas to a paper towel-lined plate and sprinkle with salt. Cook the remaining tortillas in batches, adding another 1–2 tablespoons of oil as needed.

Preheat oven to 375°F.

In a bowl, whisk together chile powder, garlic powder, and chicken stock.

Reduce heat under frying pan to medium and add back in half of the cooked tortillas. Add in 2–3 ladlefuls of flavored stock. Cook, stirring the tortillas occasionally, for 2–3 minutes, or until most of the sauce has soaked into the tortillas and evaporated. Transfer tortillas to a large baking sheet. Continue the process with the second half of tortillas.

Once all the tortillas are on the baking sheet, gently crack 5 eggs over tortillas. Bake for 12–15 minutes, or until the egg whites are cooked through and the yolks are still slightly soft.

Serve hot and top with cotija cheese, avocado, red onion, radishes, cilantro, and hot sauce.

Kale & Sausage Breakfast Pizza

2 tablespoons olive oil + more for topping

1 small russet potato, diced

Kosher salt and freshly ground black pepper

½ lb breakfast sausage

1½ cups kale, ribs removed and leaves chopped

All-purpose flour, for dusting

2 pizza dough disks (page 26)

2 cups shredded mozzarella cheese

1 cup freshly grated Parmesan cheese

1 tablespoon minced rosemary

6 eggs

2 green onions, chopped

This savory kale and sausage breakfast pizza brings me similar amounts of happiness as waking up without an alarm clock. Perfectly crispy pizza dough below, topped with classic American breakfast flavors like sausage, runny eggs, and plenty of cheese. Inspired by my lovely friend Sierra, who was born in Italy but has since turned American, much like this deliciously balanced meal.

MAKES 2 PIZZAS

In a large sauté pan over medium-high heat, heat oil. Add in potato, season with salt and pepper, and sauté for 4–5 minutes. Add in breakfast sausage, breaking it up with a wooden spoon, and cook for 4–5 minutes, or until sausage is crispy and almost cooked through. Add in kale and cook for 1–2 minutes, or until slightly wilted.

Preheat oven to 400°F. Line two baking sheets with parchment paper and set aside.

Lightly dust a clean surface with flour and roll out pizza dough disks to 12-inch rounds or rectangles, about ¼ inch thick. Transfer dough rounds to large baking sheets lined with parchment paper.

Brush each round with a drizzle of olive oil and sprinkle evenly with mozzarella cheese, Parmesan cheese, and rosemary. Divide potato-sausage mixture evenly over each pizza. Make 3 small wells in cheese topping on each pizza and crack an egg into each well. Season eggs with salt and pepper and bake in the oven for 10–15 minutes, or until pizza edges are golden brown.

Top with chopped green onions, slice, and serve.

Treat Yourself!

You know how magazines always say "Don't be afraid to buy yourself flowers"? I'd much rather treat myself with warm, fresh chocolate chip cookies—anyone else?! No matter what the occasion, dessert is always appropriate. Yellow birthday cake with chocolate frosting, duh! Peach-blueberry pie for the family barbecue, of course. A mocha almond fudge brownie and a glass of cab in the bathtub, you better believe it. I'm all about celebrating the sweet moments well, with something sweet!

Classic Birthday Cake with Chocolate Buttercream

FOR THE CAKE

Nonstick baking spray

3 cups all-purpose flour, sifted + more for pans

2 cups granulated sugar

1 cup (2 sticks) unsalted butter, at room temp

5 eggs, at room temp

1 tablespoon baking powder

½ teaspoon kosher salt

1¼ cups whole milk

2 teaspoons pure vanilla extract

½ cup rainbow sprinkles + more for topping (optional)

FOR THE BUTTERCREAM FROSTING

1½ cups (3 sticks) unsalted butter, at room temp

3–3½ cups powdered sugar

¾ cup cocoa powder

½ teaspoon kosher salt

3–4 tablespoons milk

2 teaspoons pure vanilla extract

A classic cake made for any birthday occasion. Fluffy golden funfetti layers with rich chocolate fudge frosting are topped with an obscene amount of sprinkles and plenty of candles. Don't forget to make a wish!

SERVES 10

To make the cake, preheat oven to 350°F. Coat two 9-inch round cake tins with nonstick baking spray, dust with flour, and line the bottoms with parchment paper rounds.

In the bowl of a stand mixer fitted with the paddle attachment (or in a large mixing bowl with a handheld mixer) combine sugar and butter and beat together for about 3–5 minutes, until very light and fluffy. Add in eggs, one at a time, beating well after each addition.

In a separate bowl, whisk together sifted flour, baking powder, and salt. Add flour mixture in three additions, alternating with the milk in two additions (begin and end with flour mixture), beating on low speed to incorporate each addition. Gently fold in the vanilla extract and sprinkles.

Divide batter evenly between prepared cake tins. Bake for 25–30 minutes, or until a toothpick inserted in the center comes out clean. Let cake cool in the tin for 30–40 minutes, then transfer to a wire rack to finish cooling completely.

To make the buttercream frosting, in the bowl of a stand mixer fitted with the paddle attachment (or in a large bowl with a handheld mixer), beat softened butter for about 2–3 minutes, until light and fluffy. In a medium bowl, whisk together 3 cups powdered sugar, cocoa powder, and salt. Add 1 cup of powdered sugar mixture at a time to batter, followed by 1 tablespoon milk, beating on low after each addition. If frosting is on the thicker side, add in more milk as needed; if buttercream is too thin, add remaining ½ cup of powdered sugar. Beat in vanilla extract.

To assemble the cake, trim away the domed top of each cake layer with a serrated knife. Place the first cake layer onto a serving platter or cake stand. Spread an even layer of frosting on the cake and top with second cake layer. Spread remaining buttercream on the top and sides of the cake evenly. Garnish with extra sprinkles, if desired.

Key Lime Rum Tart

FOR THE CRUST

2 cups graham cracker crumbs

⅓ cup granulated sugar

½ teaspoon cinnamon

½ teaspoon kosher salt

½ cup (1 stick) unsalted butter, melted

FOR THE FILLING

1 can (14 oz) condensed milk

⅔ cup fresh Key lime or lime juice, strained (about 20–40 Key limes or 6–8 regular limes)

4 large egg yolks

3 tablespoons white rum

FOR THE TOPPING

1 cup heavy cream

2 tablespoons white rum

¼ cup granulated sugar

Lime zest, for garnish

Lime wheels, for garnish

One bite of this tart and you'll instantly feel like you've been transported somewhere warm and tropical. Each creamy slice is bursting with tart lime flavor on top of an extra-thick graham cracker crust. Be sure to serve it up with extra rum-infused whipped cream. This tart makes a bit more than a regular Key lime pie, perfect for serving after a small dinner party.

SERVES 6-8

To make the crust, in a medium bowl, stir together graham cracker crumbs, granulated sugar, cinnamon, salt, and melted butter until combined.

Preheat oven to 350°F.

Press the crust mixture into the bottom and sides of an 8½ x 11-inch rectangular tart pan. Place tart pan on a baking sheet and bake crust for 10–12 minutes, or until lightly browned and fragrant. Remove tart pan from oven and place on a rack to cool while you prepare tart filling.

To make the tart filling, in a large bowl, whisk together condensed milk, lime juice, egg yolks, and white rum until smooth. Pour filling into cooled tart crust and return tart (on baking sheet) to oven. Bake for 20–25 minutes, or until edges are set and center still jiggles slightly when pan is shaken. Remove tart from oven and let cool to room temperature. Refrigerate tart overnight or at least for several hours before serving.

To make the topping, in the bowl of a stand mixer fitted with the whisk attachment (or in a large mixing bowl with a handheld mixer), combine heavy cream, white rum, and sugar. Whip on high speed until stiff peaks form when whisk is lifted.

Once the tart has chilled, top with swirls of whipped cream and garnish with lime wheels and fresh zest.

Miso Dark Chocolate Chip Cookies

1½ cups all-purpose flour

¾ teaspoon baking soda

¼ teaspoon kosher salt

¾ cup (1½ sticks) unsalted butter (divided)

1 cup brown sugar

¼ cup granulated sugar

1 egg, at room temp

2 egg yolks

2 tablespoons white miso paste

1 teaspoon pure vanilla extract

6 oz bittersweet chocolate bar, chopped

I can hear it now. *Another chocolate chip cookie recipe?* I promise, these hit differently. Sweet, with rich dark chocolate chips, and salty, with an extremely interesting depth of flavor from the miso paste. Perfectly crisp on the outside and gooey on the inside. Inspired by a cookie shop, Creme, in London, these are an addicting favorite that make many (probably too many) appearances at my house.

SERVES 8

Preheat oven to 375°F. Line two baking sheets with parchment and set aside.

In a large bowl, whisk together flour, baking soda, and salt and set aside.

In a heavy-bottomed saucepan over medium heat, melt half the butter (6 tablespoons). Swirl until it starts to turn a light amber color. Be careful! The butter can burn very easily. Pour butter from pan into a large glass bowl to cool. Once butter has cooled slightly, add in remaining butter to melt together.

Whisk brown sugar, granulated sugar, egg, and egg yolks into cooled melted butter until smooth. Whisk in miso paste and vanilla extract. Add dry ingredients to wet ingredients and fold batter together. Fold in the dark chocolate; do not overmix.

Scoop 2- to 3-tablespoon balls of cookie dough and place onto prepared baking sheets. Bake cookies for 8–10 minutes, or until edges are golden brown. Cookies will continue to cook outside of oven; do not overbake.

Let cookies cool on pan for 10 minutes before transferring to a wire rack to cool completely.

Mocha Almond Fudge Brownies

¾ cup (1½ sticks) unsalted butter, melted + more for pan

8 oz good-quality semisweet chocolate, chopped (divided)

¾ cup granulated sugar

½ cup brown sugar

2 eggs, at room temp

1 teaspoon pure vanilla extract

1 tablespoon instant espresso powder

¾ cup all-purpose flour

¼ cup cocoa powder

1 teaspoon kosher salt

½ cup chopped almonds + more for topping (optional)

These brownies are inspired by my love affair with mocha almond fudge ice cream from Rite Aid (formerly known as Thrifty's). Their ice cream is totally underrated and completely delicious. A rich espresso aroma imbues this brownie batter studded with fudgy chocolate pieces and roasted almonds. Make these extremely rich brownies for a chocolate lover in your life—or take a slice in with you for an extra-decadent bubble bath.

SERVES 9

Preheat oven to 350°F. Line an 8-inch square baking dish with parchment paper, grease with butter, and set aside.

Put about three-quarters (6 oz) of the chopped chocolate in a microwave-safe bowl. Microwave in 15-second intervals, stirring after each interval, until chocolate has melted. Set aside to cool.

In a separate large bowl, combine melted butter and granulated and brown sugars and whisk together until mixture is light and fluffy. Add eggs and vanilla to the butter mixture and whisk until combined. Slowly whisk in the cooled melted chocolate. Sift in the espresso powder, flour, cocoa powder, and salt. Fold brownie batter until wet ingredients are just incorporated into dry ingredients; do not overmix.

Gently fold in almonds and transfer mixture to prepared baking dish. Top with remaining chocolate chunks and bake for 25–30 minutes for a fudgy brownie and 30–35 minutes for a more cake-like brownie. Let brownies cool completely, top with almonds (if using), slice into 9 even squares, and serve.

Nanna's Coconut Cream Cake

FOR THE COCONUT SIMPLE SYRUP

1 cup water

½ cup sugar

2 teaspoons coconut extract

¾ cup sweetened shredded coconut

FOR THE CAKE

¾ cup (1½ sticks) unsalted butter, at room temp + more for pan

2 cups all-purpose flour

2¼ teaspoons baking powder

½ teaspoon salt

1½ cups granulated sugar

5 large egg whites

1 teaspoon pure vanilla extract

2 teaspoons coconut extract

½ cup sour cream

1 cup canned unsweetened coconut milk

¾ cup sweetened shredded coconut

FOR THE FROSTING

1 cup (2 sticks) unsalted butter, at room temp

1 package (8 oz) cream cheese, at room temp

1 teaspoon pure vanilla extract

2 teaspoons coconut extract

1 teaspoon kosher salt

3–4 cups powdered sugar

3 tablespoons canned unsweetened coconut milk

2 cups sweetened coconut chips, toasted

Every September my dearest Nanna requests a coconut cake for her birthday. Tender coconut-infused cake layers soaked in coconut syrup give it a supremely moist texture. Each layer and the outside are frosted with an intensely infused creamy coconut buttercream, and it's sprinkled off with toasted coconut.

SERVES 10

To make the coconut simple syrup, in a small saucepan over medium heat, combine water and sugar. Heat until sugar dissolves and mixture is clear. Remove from heat, add in coconut extract and sweetened coconut shreds, and let mixture steep for at least 30–60 minutes. Strain out coconut shreds and reserve syrup for cake layers.

Preheat oven to 350°F and butter and line three 8-inch round cake tins.

To make the cake, in a large bowl, sift together flour, baking powder, and salt and set aside. In the bowl of a stand mixer fitted with the paddle attachment (or in a large bowl with a handheld mixer), beat softened butter and sugar on high for 2–3 minutes, until pale and fluffy. Beat egg whites into butter mixture until just combined. Add in vanilla extract, coconut extract, and sour cream until just combined.

Add the flour mixture to the batter in two additions, each followed by half the coconut milk, beating after each addition. Fold in coconut shreds, then divide batter evenly among cake tins. Bake for 20–25 minutes, or until a toothpick inserted in the centers of the cakes comes out clean. Let cake layers cool completely on wire racks before assembling.

Meanwhile, make the frosting. In the bowl of a stand mixer fitted with the paddle attachment, beat softened butter and cream cheese together for 2–3 minutes, or until light and fluffy. Add in vanilla extract, coconut extract, and salt. While mixer is running on low, add 1 cup of powdered sugar at a time. As frosting begins to thicken, add in 1 tablespoon coconut milk at a time until frosting reaches a spreadable consistency.

To assemble the cake, place the first layer of cake onto a cake stand. Brush on an even layer of coconut simple syrup. Spread an even layer of frosting over the first cake layer and stack the next layer, brushing with syrup and spreading with frosting. Place the last cake layer upside down for a flat top. Brush with syrup, then spread remaining frosting all over the cake top and down the sides, frosting evenly. Cover sides of cake with toasted sweetened coconut chips.

Peach-Blueberry Pie

FOR THE CRUST

2½ cups all-purpose flour
+ more for dusting

1 tablespoon granulated sugar

½ teaspoon kosher salt

1 cup (2 sticks) cold unsalted butter

¼ cup ice water

FOR THE FILLING

6–7 ripe peaches

5–6 oz (1½ cups) blueberries

⅔ cup granulated sugar

2 teaspoons cinnamon

Zest of 1 lemon

1 tablespoon fresh lemon juice

5 tablespoons cornstarch

1 egg

1 tablespoon milk

Vanilla ice cream, for serving

My most requested dessert? This peach-blueberry pie. Seriously. Each year I get asked to make this iconic summer favorite. If I'm being really honest with you, I stole this recipe idea from a really rich lady from NYC at a family friend's farm picnic in Pennsylvania one year. After failing to track down the recipe, I resorted to a re-creation. My first bite of this was under a huge tree on a hot summer day. I remember the fruit filling was laced with cinnamon, sweet peach flavor, and bursting blueberries in each bite. Pile each slice with a huge scoop of vanilla ice cream for the ultimate summer treat.

SERVES 8

To make the crust, in a large bowl, combine flour, sugar, and salt. With a box grater, shred your 2 sticks butter into flour mixture. With a pastry blender or rubbing with your fingertips, blend butter and flour until a crumbly texture forms. Slowly add in your ice water 1–2 tablespoons at a time, incorporating with your hands after each pour. The dough can vary in consistency because of climate (if you live in a dry climate, you may need a little more water, or less in a humid climate). When dough is ready, it will come together in a rough ball; do not overmix.

Form dough into two disks, wrap in plastic wrap, and refrigerate for at least 2 hours and up to 1 day. Roll one dough disk out on a well-floured surface. The dough may seem tough to roll out, but apply pressure. You want the dough to stay cold, or it will be difficult to move into pie dish. Roll your 11-inch dough round around your rolling pin and unroll over your pie dish. Set aside.

Preheat oven to 350°F. To make the filling, bring a medium-sized pot of water to a rolling boil. In a large bowl, prepare an ice bath. Score your peaches with a paring knife by putting a small slit in the bottom and top of the peach. This slit will help the peeling process. Drop half the peaches in boiling water for about 2 minutes. Drop the peaches into ice bath to stop the cooking. Repeat with the remaining peaches. Peel the peaches, using a paring knife if necessary.

Cut peeled peaches into slices and toss with blueberries, sugar, cinnamon, lemon zest and juice, and cornstarch. Pour into uncooked pie shell. Roll out your other dough disk and create the top of the pie with a design or lattice of your choice. Whisk egg and milk together to make an egg wash and brush over top of pie with a pastry brush.

Place pie on a baking sheet and bake pie for 50–60 minutes, or until fruit is bubbling and crust is golden brown. If edges begin to burn, tent with aluminum foil. Let pie cool for 20–30 minutes, and serve warm with vanilla ice cream.

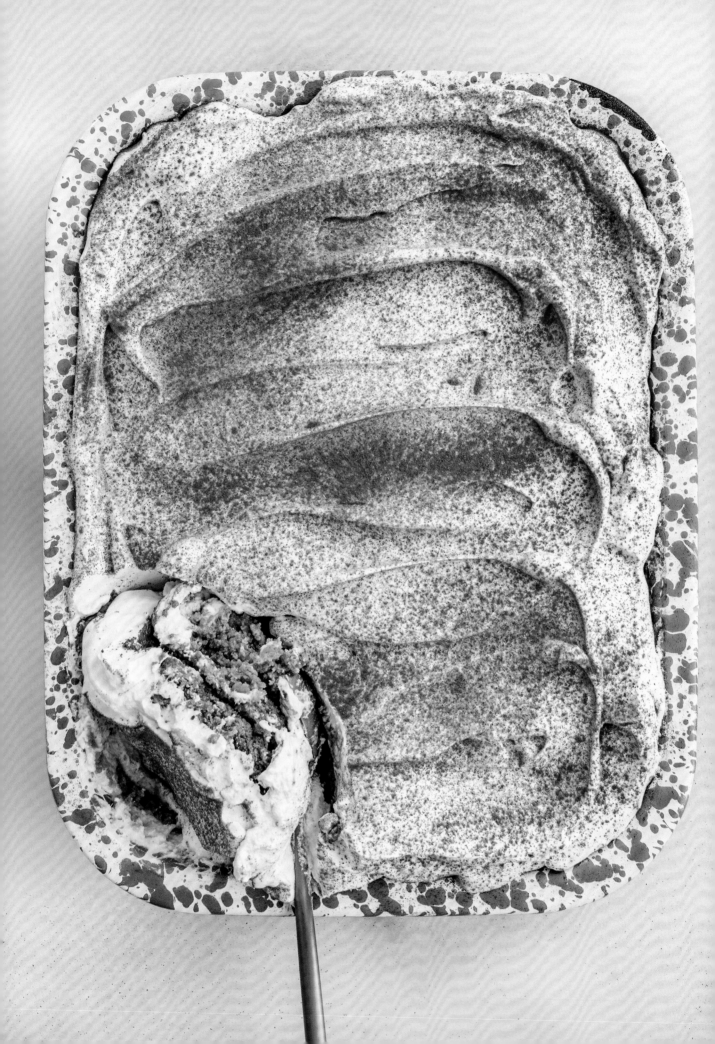

Snickerdoodle Milk & Cookie Tiramisu

FOR THE SNICKERDOODLES

1 cup (2 sticks) butter, at room temp

¾ cup granulated sugar

½ cup light brown sugar

1 egg

1 egg yolk

2 teaspoons pure vanilla extract

2¾ cups all-purpose flour

1 teaspoon baking soda

1 teaspoon cream of tartar

½ teaspoon kosher salt

1 teaspoon cinnamon

FOR THE CINNAMON SUGAR

¼ cup granulated sugar

1 tablespoon cinnamon

FOR THE TIRAMISU

1 cup fresh hot coffee or espresso, at room temp

2 tablespoons Kahlúa

2 tablespoons brown sugar

1 teaspoon milk or half-and-half

2 cups heavy cream

2 containers (8 oz each) mascarpone cheese, at room temp

2 teaspoons pure vanilla extract

⅔ cup granulated sugar

Ground cinnamon, for dusting

Pinch of salt

A freshly baked cookie and hot coffee are high up on my dessert list. This tiramisu is the best of both worlds. Inspired by the classic, but made with sweet snickerdoodles and topped with light layers of rich cinnamon.

SERVES 6–8

To make the snickerdoodles, preheat oven to 325°F. Line two baking sheets with parchment paper and set aside.

In the bowl of a stand mixer fitted with the paddle attachment beat the softened butter, granulated sugar, and brown sugar on medium-high speed for about 3–5 minutes, or until light and fluffy. Stir in egg, egg yolk, and vanilla extract until just incorporated.

In a separate large bowl, whisk together flour, baking soda, cream of tartar, salt, and cinnamon. Turn mixer speed to low and slowly add flour mixture to butter mixture until incorporated, scraping down the sides of the bowl with a rubber spatula as necessary.

To make the cinnamon sugar, in a small bowl, mix together sugar and cinnamon. Scoop 2 tablespoons of cookie dough and roll into a ball. Dip dough balls into cinnamon sugar and place onto the baking sheet 2 inches apart. Gently flatten cookie tops down slightly. You will need 18 cookies for the tiramisu. Bake cookies for 10–12 minutes, or until the tops look slightly cracked. Let cool for 5 minutes on the baking sheet, then transfer to a wire rack to finish cooling.

To make the tiramisu, pour cooled coffee into a medium bowl. Mix in Kahlúa, brown sugar, and milk and set aside. In the bowl of a stand mixer fitted with the whisk attachment whip the heavy cream on high until slightly stiff peaks begin to form when the whisk is lifted (do not overmix). Add in mascarpone cheese and vanilla extract, granulated sugar, and salt. Whip until smooth and fluffy.

Quickly submerge 18 snickerdoodle cookies into the coffee mixture. Do not to oversaturate. Arrange 6 cookies into an even layer in a small casserole dish and sift with a light layer of ground cinnamon. Spread one-third of the cream mixture over the first layer of the snickerdoodles and repeat the process 2 more times. Cover tiramisu and refrigerate for 2–4 hours. You can serve right away, but the chilling time will provide more depth of flavor and a luxurious creamy texture.

Dust the top with a very light layer of ground cinnamon and a pinch of salt before serving.

Peanut Butter-Chocolate Chip Skillet Cookie à la Mode

1 cup (2 sticks) unsalted butter + more for pan

2½ cups all-purpose flour

1 teaspoon baking soda

1 teaspoon kosher salt

1 egg, at room temp

1½ cups light brown sugar

3 teaspoons pure vanilla extract

1 cup dark chocolate chunks + more for top

1 cup crushed pretzels + more for top

½ cup creamy peanut butter + more for top

Vanilla ice cream, for serving

Pizookie, skillet cookie, whatever you want to call it, it's freaking delicious. This jumbo-size gooey chocolate chip skillet cookie literally oozes with peanut butter and pretzels for the most marvelous sweet and salty flavor mash-up. I've never served it with bowls, only spoons, and it's usually gone within ten minutes flat. Time it.

SERVES 4–5

In a heavy-bottomed saucepan over medium heat, melt and swirl butter until it starts to turn a light amber color. Be careful! The butter can burn very easily. Remove the butter from the heat and pour into a large glass bowl to cool. While butter is cooling, prepare the rest of the dough.

Preheat oven to 350°F. Grease a 9-inch cast-iron frying pan with butter or nonstick spray.

In a large bowl, whisk together flour, baking soda, and salt and set aside. Add egg, brown sugar, and vanilla extract to the cooled brown butter and whisk together. Add the wet ingredient mixture to the flour mixture and fold to combine. Add in chocolate chunks and pretzel pieces and fold again.

Press half of the cookie dough mixture into the frying pan and dollop the peanut butter evenly around it. Top with remaining cookie dough. Dollop a few more teaspoons of peanut butter on top, and scatter extra chocolate chunks and extra crushed pretzels.

Bake for 20–25 minutes, or until top is golden brown. Top with vanilla ice cream before serving.

Strawberry-Fig Galette

1 pie dough disk (page 242)

All-purpose flour, for dusting

2 cups sliced strawberries

6–8 figs, sliced

¼ cup sugar + more for topping

2 tablespoons melted butter

Zest of 1 lemon

1 egg

Whipped cream or vanilla ice cream, for serving

A galette is one of those desserts that sounds really fancy when you serve it, but will actually take you fifteen minutes to put together. It's a secret-weapon dessert that I pull out when I have lots of fresh produce and need something quick. I always keep extra pie dough in my freezer for such occasions. Toss in any of your favorite fruit combos and serve with whipped cream or vanilla ice cream.

SERVES 6

Preheat oven to 375°F. Line a large baking sheet with parchment paper and set aside.

Roll out the pie dough disk on a well-floured surface. The dough may seem tough to roll out, but apply pressure. Roll your dough into a 11-inch round. Slide dough onto prepared baking sheet.

In a small bowl, mix together strawberries, figs, sugar, melted butter, and lemon zest. Place the fruit evenly on the pie dough round, leaving a 2-inch border around the edges for folding.

Fold in the edges of the galette to create a decorative overlapping border for the fruit. Lightly beat 1 egg and brush onto the edges of the galette. Sprinkle dough with sugar.

Bake for 40–45 minutes, or until fruit is bubbling and crust is golden brown. Serve warm, with a dollop of whipped cream or ice cream.

Index

Acknowledgments

To my blog readers, Instagram followers, and beyond, this book is just as much yours as it is mine. Thank you for making my recipes and sharing my blog with your friends and family. I wish I could take each one of you out for a margarita! I feel so fortunate and humble to have a job that I love, and I owe that to each and every one of you.

Mom, thank you for your endless amounts of love and being my number one cheerleader. Growing up I watched you make such wonderful holiday dinners, you have taught me what it means to "entertain every day" and care for people at your table. You always made people in our home feel special, and I'm always striving to do the same.

Dad, my life advisor, my friend, my rock. Anything I do, I do with you in mind. Thank you for always being right by my side, pushing me to be my best, no matter what I was interested in. I owe any bit of success in life to you, and I'm always striving to make you proud. #bloghard

Ralph, thank you so much for being a loving, supporting, and hilarious brother. You are the comedic relief everyone needs in life.

Jared & Rascal, my boys, you are my home and my safe haven. Thank you for your constant love and support through this wacky adventure of following my dreams. For being the best taste-testers I could ever ask for.

Nanna, thank you for constantly encouraging me to grow and become the best woman I can be. I'll never stop telling myself that "you have to have a dream, to make a dream come true." Also, thank you for always telling me to recognize bullshit, for bullshit. It's a very valuable life lesson.

Abbie, my right-hand lady. I don't think this book would be here without you. You are SO insanely talented, endlessly creative, and ready with a *touch* of sass for the perfect combo.

To the incredible people at Weldon Owen, Amy, Chrissy, Ashley, Jourdan, thank you so much for allowing this dream of mine to become a reality. It's been such a joy and a privilege to create something so wonderful with you.

My book agent Anna, thank you for sticking with me and finding the absolute perfect fit for this book! Jackie Segedin and everyone at the Cook It Agency, thank you for your constant support!

My photo-shoot A-Team that rented that crazy house for the book shoot. Abbie, Constance, Alex, Sabrina, Taylor, Kelly, Koko, Sierra, Evan, Jackie, and Jared. Thank you so much for not only coming (looking gorgeous btw) but for being models and helping me clean after the longest of days. I am forever grateful. Bernadette, for making me feel beautiful and being such a gem. Constance, thank you for taking on this photography mission with us and creating some of my favorite images of all time. #withalittlehelpfrommyfriends.

My recipe testers: Lauren and Dave Creel, Kathy Mathe, Jess Larson, Anna Fatlowitz, Mariah Rickard, Ranleigh Starling, Carita Fambro. Thank you SO much for testing and helping me make these recipes perfect.

My friends and family for your endless support. Alex and Sabrina, my ladies, my best friends. Thank you for always keeping it real with me, you've always had my back and I'll always have yours. Sabrina, thank you for my amazing striped red manicure seen throughout the book. #iconic Katie, quite often I found myself seeing you as my muse for this book. Talking through recipes, seeing you cook them for friends, you're a constant light of inspiration for me. Sierra aka #myworkwife, my mentor, and my hot Italian Stallion, I am grateful for your wisdom, banter, and friendship.

Mr. Hiben & Mrs. Kachaenchai, my two most important educators. Thank you for taking a chance on a 16-year-old me and giving me a platform to discover my love for photography and what it meant to work extremely hard.

To anyone who has tried a recipe, helped me spread the word about my blog, or supported this journey. There are so many of you, and from the bottom of my heart, thank you!

XOXO EVL

EVERYDAY ENTERTAINING

Conceived and produced by Weldon Owen International

A WELDON OWEN PRODUCTION

PO Box 3088
San Rafael, CA 94912
www.weldonowen.com

Copyright ©2021 Weldon Owen
All rights reserved, including the right of reproduction
in whole or in part in any form.

Printed in China
10 9 8 7 6 5 4 3 2

Library of Congress
Cataloging-in-Publication data is available.

ISBN: 978-1-68188-588-9

WELDON OWEN INTERNATIONAL

CEO Raoul Goff
Publisher Roger Shaw
Associate Publisher Amy Marr
Editorial Assistant Jourdan Plautz
Creative Director Chrissy Kwasnik
Designer Ashley Quackenbush
Production Manager Eden Orlesky

Photography Elizabeth Van Lierde, Abagail Halstead
Additional photography Constance Mariena pages (1,2,
6,8,14,44,45,53,57,68,92,96,114,116,118,123,168,170,175,185,
188,199,202,204,206,220,224,228,236,255)
Food Stylng Elizabeth Van Lierde, Abagail Halsted

Weldon Owen wishes to thank the following for
their generous support in producing this book:
Sarah Putman Clegg, Rachel Markowitz, and Elizabeth Parson.